6.99 ✓

ONE HUNDRED HILL WALKS FROM LIVERPOOL

ONE HUNDRED HILL WALKS FROM LIVERPOOL

The Essential Guide to Hill Walking from Merseyside

JIM GRINDLE

Series Editor
John S. Chalmers

MAINSTREAM
PUBLISHING

EDINBURGH AND LONDON

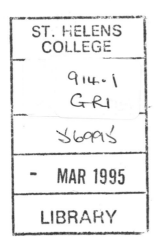
The moral right of the author has been asserted

First published in Great Britain in 1993 by
MAINSTREAM PUBLISHING COMPANY
(EDINBURGH) LTD
7 Albany Street
Edinburgh EH1 3UG
ISBN 1 85158 524 9

A catalogue record for this book is available from the British
Library

Phototypeset in Times by Intype, London
Printed in Great Britain by The Cromwell Press, Melksham,
Wiltshire

CONTENTS

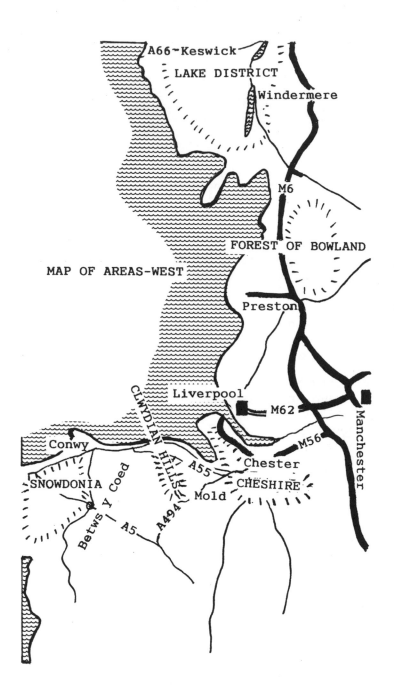

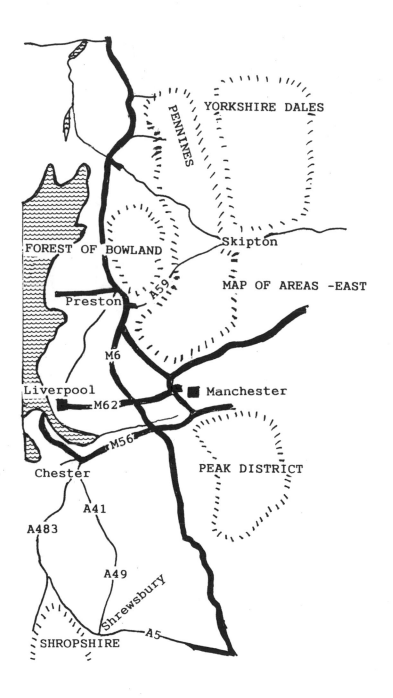

ABOUT THIS BOOK

There is a large and growing number of walking and rambling clubs in Liverpool and Merseyside. Planning and leading walks, however, tends to be left to the minority who have enough experience of the various hill areas within reach. This book is a practical guide to be used in planning and when on the hills and it will be of use to those who aspire to leadership within their club as much as to those who wish to branch out on their own.

While there are few really good hills within close reach of Liverpool, it is very easy to get to most of the major mountain areas of northern England if you are prepared to drive for a few hours. It is worth underlining the obvious: that by leaving early and coming back late a lot of heavy motorway traffic can be avoided (except when the Blackpool lights are on) and that there are far fewer walkers out on Saturdays than on Sundays.

The book contains a variety of walks which will enable you to select, according to the season, the distance to be travelled, the amount of climbing involved and the length of the walk. Most walks can be shortened and notes tell you how to do this. As far as is known, all the walks are on rights of way or on established routes. In a few cases the permission of the landowner or his agent has been obtained to cross private land. Waymarking outside National Parks or away from National Trails is patchy, particularly in the lowland areas that are sometimes used to make a circular walk. In these cases more detail is given in the text and you will find that stiles are often the surest guide. With experience it becomes easier to pick out the route of a little-used path and then to transfer this skill to devising your own route or variation.

Indeed, the author hopes that the reader will reach that stage of independence where a map and compass alone are the keys to exploring routes in less frequented areas, with all the personal satisfaction that this can bring. If that is not your aim, the book will still help you to enjoy some of the wildest and most beautiful scenery in Wales and north-west England.

ACKNOWLEDGMENTS

Coming, as I do, from south-east England, walking and climbing were recreations that I never met until a commercial appointment brought me to Liverpool. I owe a life-long debt to Fred Smith who ran courses in mountaincraft and rock-climbing as part of the city's Further Education programme. Like all other walkers I am indebted to the Ramblers' Association who have always been in the forefront of keeping the paths open and to the YHA whose doorsteps I still occasionally darken.

For this volume I would like to thank Arthur Pugh of Formby for his assistance with the photographs and the Southport group of the Ramblers' Association for their companionship on the hills. My greatest thanks and gratitude, though, are to my wife, June, who has shared the discomforts of tracing unused footpaths on occasion but who has not had the company she anticipated on my early retirement. I hope now to rescue her, the house and the garden from neglect.

NOTES

1. The sketch maps provide a quick visual idea of each walk. They are not to scale and do not replace the Ordnance Survey maps, the appropriate sheet of which should always be used. The 1:50,000 Landranger series or the 1:25,000 Outdoor Leisure series, where available, are recommended. The relevant maps for each walk are noted at the beginning of each description. Occasionally a route will require two maps.

2. The "Distance from city centre" is as it says, but double the distance for the round trip. The distances are from Liverpool; if you travel from elsewhere on Merseyside you will make your own adjustments.

3. The "Walking distance" includes an allowance for the continuous variations from the route as it would be measured on the map. It is always necessary on a hill walk to make short detours to avoid bog, rocks, hillocks etc. Even with this allowance, the resultant figure must be approximate.

4. The "Amount of climbing" is the sum of all the uphill sections of the route.

5. Distances given within the text are approximations meant for guidance only.

6. Compass directions and bearings given in the text are based on Ordnance Survey grid north. The prevailing

magnetic variation in the area is about 5° and a reading taken from the map should be increased by this amount.

7. Conditions in the countryside change and not all changes are recorded even on the Ordnance Survey maps; forests are planted or felled, new fences erected etc., so you may find some variations from what is written in the text, but these should not prevent you from finding a way round them. While every endeavour has been made to be accurate in all details, should some errors have crept in I can only apologise for these in advance. No responsibility can be accepted for any loss etc. caused by an inaccuracy, and the fact that a walk is described in this book does not imply a right of way nor does it guarantee that access will always be available.

8. A few of the walks, particularly in the Derbyshire dales, are not strictly *on* hills but they are among them and of the type which hillwalkers will enjoy, perhaps being kept for days when bad weather makes it pointless to walk on the higher fells.

9. Feedback from the user on changes that have been found, suspected inaccuracies or directions that did not seem clear, would be valuable and may be sent via the publisher.

ABBREVIATIONS

km	kilometres
ml	miles
m	metres
ft	feet
yd	yards
N, S, E, W	directions of the compass
SD-, SE-, SJ-, SO-etc	National Grid reference
TP	triangulation pillar
J-	motorway junction number-
OL	Outdoor Leisure map

WELSH PLACE NAMES

This glossary with its notes is intended to help the non-Welsh speaker to come to terms with what often appears baffling. The fluent speaker of *yr hen iaith* will excuse the simplification and omissions.

Pronunciation

With few exceptions Welsh is phonetic. In general, stress words on the last syllable but one, e.g. *Llandúdno*.

Vowels: a, e, i, o and u have long and short versions all of which are found in English; w is also a vowel, long as in "room" or short as in "put"; y is a vowel, often very short like "er" on the end of English words, e.g. "together".

Consonants: most consonants are like English. However, note: ch is like Liverpudlian "ck", as in "whacker" or like Scottish "loch", never as in "cheese"; dd is like "th" as in "that"; "f" is like "v", as in "over"; "ff" is like "f" as in "offer"; "ll" has a sound which does not exist in English – it is like "l" but without using the voice and needs to be taught or picked up through practice; "s" is like "s" in "soft" not as in "laser"; "th" is like "th" in "thumb" not as in "they".

In Welsh many words change their initial sound

depending on circumstances. In place names you will find many examples of this – pont/bont, moel/foel, bach/fach, for instance.

Glossary

aber	river mouth	llwyd	grey
afon	river	llyn	lake
allt	wooded hillside	maen	stone
bach	little	maes	field
bron	hillside	melyn	yellow
bryn	hill	mor	sea
bwlch	a pass	mynydd	mountain
cae	field	nant	stream
caer	camp or fort	ogof	cave
canol	middle	pen	top
carn(edd)	cairn, hill	pentref	village
carreg	stone	pistyll	waterfall
cefn	ridge	pont	bridge
clogwyn	cliff	pwll	pool
coch	red	rhos	moor
coed	wood	rhyd	ford
crib	ridge	tan	under
cwm	valley	tref	town
du	black	ty	house
dyffryn	valley	tyddyn	croft
eglwys	church	uchaf	upper
ffordd	road	wen	white
foel	bare hill	y/yr	the
glas	blue	yn	in
glyn	valley	ynys	island
hafod	summer dwelling		
hen	old		
hendref	winter dwelling		
hir	long		
isaf	lower		
llan	church		

15

SYMBOLS ON SKETCH MAPS

P	Parking place/start of walk
↑ N	North
⟶	Route of walk
⟹	Uphill
▭	Building
⊥▢	Church
(woodland symbol)	Woodland
(water symbol)	Water
o	Hilltop
△	Triangulation pillar
(crag symbol)	Rock outcrop or crag
⇑	Power line
⅄	Television mast
(site symbol)	Archaeological site
＋＋＋＋	Railway

THE WALKS

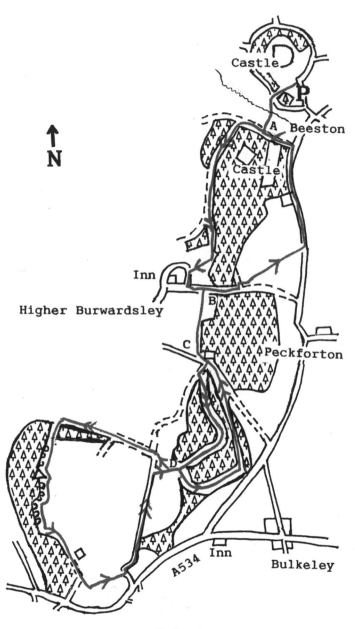

N

Castle

Beeston

A

Castle

P

Inn

Higher Burwardsley

B

C

Peckforton

D

A534 Inn

Bulkeley

Walk 1

CHESHIRE AND MERSEYSIDE

1. *The Peckforton Hills*

Ordnance Survey Map No: 117
Distance from city centre: 53km/33ml
Walking distance: 15km/9ml
Amount of climbing: 300m/1000ft
 A walk for all seasons in an area with particular charms in autumn because of the abundance of trees. Watch in particular for the sweet chestnuts. Beeston Castle dates from 1337 and is worth a visit, as is nearby Peckforton Castle. An impressive 19th-century sham, it was used as a setting for the most recent Robin Hood film. Views of the Welsh hills are outstanding.
 Park near Beeston Castle. SJ539580. To get there take A591 to Runcorn. Cross bridge to Widnes and follow A557/A56 to Frodsham. Turn left on B5152 to Delamere and cross A556 and A54. At junction with A49 turn right and at bottom of hill, left on Tarporley bypass. Turn right by inn at traffic lights and follow tourist signs to Beeston Castle. Carpark is in picnic area on left on bend. (Larger carpark on right opposite gate-house, is for visitors to castle.)
 First half of walk follows Sandstone Trail; waymark, sole of boot with S on. From carpark turn immediately left on Trail which goes downhill through small wood

to lane. Cross and go half left across field through crops (path usually left clear), cross stream and go by field edge to next lane (point A). Turn right.

After 200m/220yd go through gateway on left on to stony track following right-hand edge of wood. At next gate continue ahead where lanes cross. When lane starts to go down, turn up to left on steeper path and at top turn right. Go through gate into field and at lane turn left (right for village and inn). Go left again at T-junction and after 50m/55yd cross stile on right into field (point B). Follow stiles through to next lane. Turn left and almost immediately right on to stony lane opposite sandstone estate lodge (point C). After 100m/110yd turn left at Trail sign up stone steps leading to path curving right through woods on Bulkeley Hill. Path keeps to top of steep slope left and leaves wood by gate (point D).

After 100m/110yd path goes half right across field to lane. Cross and go along stony track opposite. Where this bends left continue ahead on smaller path on right-hand edge of wood. Track rises over cliffs to TP. Follow trail signs downhill past farm and on track. Where this bends right continue ahead on path at sign-post to Coppermines. After 75m/80yd turn left through stile at signpost to Poacher Inn. Easily followed path leads to lane (note copper mine chimney on right). Turn left.

After 600m/660yd cross stile on right between iron gates and follow field edge to reach point D again. Turn right at signpost to Bulkeley village. Track leads downhill to lane. At lane stay inside wood and turn left at signpost to Peckforton Gap.

Cross private road and keep on main track. Note on each side of track tramlines laid to assist building of water pipeline. As track rises to Gap another track from right converges at lodge at point C. Turn right over stile past lodge to retrace steps to point B. Turn right. Track becomes cobbled. Beeston is signposted on left along track to left and then immediately right again to continue in same direction and then half left over stiles through crops down to lane. Turn left.

After 1.2km/0.75ml turn left on minor lane to reach point A. Turn right and retrace steps back to carpark.

This walk can be shortened (a) by continuing E on reaching point B (saving 7.2km/4.5ml), or (b) by turning left on reaching point D (saving 4.5km/2.8ml).

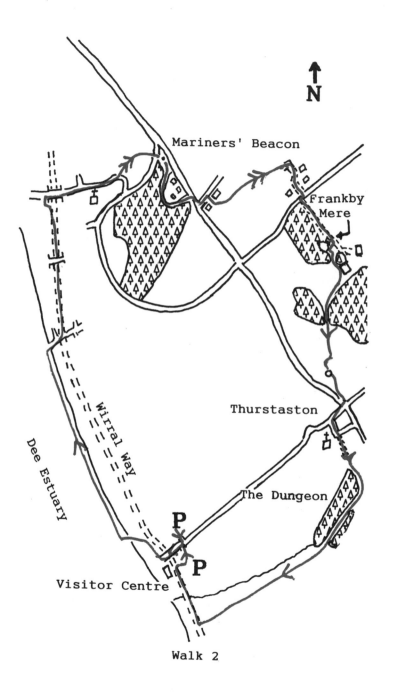

Mariners' Beacon

Frankby Mere

Dee Estuary

Wirral Way

Thurstaston

The Dungeon

P

P

Visitor Centre

Walk 2

N

2. Thurstaston Hill

Ordnance Survey Map No: 108
Distance from city centre: 27km/16ml
Walking distance: 13km/8ml
Amount of climbing: 93m/307ft

This walk combines three areas of open countryside into a walk of reasonable length, given the urban surroundings. The views from these modest heights are excellent, particularly towards Wales.

Park at the Wirral Country Park Visitor Centre, Thurstaston. SJ238834.

To get there take the Wallasey Tunnel, M53 to J3 and A552/A551 (Heswall). After 1.2km/0.75ml turn right at small roundabout on to B5138 and immediately right to Irby. At T-junction turn right and at crossroads with A540 go straight across. Turn right at T-junction and road leads to Country Park. Carparks are on both sides of road.

Return to road from carpark, walk right to end at metal barrier. Turn right and follow waymarking for 100m/110yd until steps on left lead down to beach. (If tide is in follow Wirral Way from car parking area.) Turn right and walk along beach past cliffs and concrete ramp of Dee Sailing Club until reaching sandstone wall. Go up steps to road, between buttresses of former railway bridge, and turn immediately left into carpark. Pick up footpath left.

At second bridge go left to road, turn right to cross bridge and pass church on right. Cross road and on bend take footpath on left between stone walls. Cross minor road and go up steps to Mariners' Beacon on Caldy Hill.

Take footpath on right going SE and stay on this high path to Paton's monument and viewfinder (if in doubt take left-hand forks). Continue on main path with houses now visible on left through trees. Path curves left to sandstone wall. Go through gap and across bridleway through gap in far wall. Take right-hand fork. Fork right again. Path curves left to pass

23

tennis court on right and begins to descend. Cross end of drive with bridleway on left and continue on path opposite at back of houses on right until open fields are visible. Turn left at bench with sandstone base and walk with fields on right to steps down to A540.

Cross road, turn right and then left along Grange Cross Lane. Take Frankby footpath on right between houses. Follow path through fields and along lane which bends between houses to B5140. Turn right and after 100m/110yd cross at public footpath sign into Royden Park.

After 100m/110yd take path on right opposite field gate on left (note low signpost for self-guided walk 1). Turn left at T-junction (No 1) by Frankby Mere and left again (No 1) after 20m/22yd to cross S in front of Tudor house. Once past house turn half-right across open ground to opening in large sandstone wall. From here go along main path S with occasional sandstone markers (BS). When end of wall is reached on left, go half-right at stone boundary marker on to solid stone path. At huge outcrop (Thor's Stone) turn right to top of low crags and then left to TP and viewfinder. Main track is now SE down to carpark by A540. Turn left through picnic area, cross road by inn and go down Station Road. At T-junction turn left to pass church on right. When lane bends left go straight on along lane which becomes footpath.

After 1km/0.7ml a wood is reached – the Dungeon! Turn right and follow path downhill, crossing stream several times. At T-junction go down left to stream again. To view cave, gorge and waterfall turn left and return. Follow path SW to Wirral Way. Turn right and walk 1km/0.7ml to carpark.

This walk may be shortened slightly by returning directly to the carpark from Station Road. Save 2km/1.2ml.

Walk 3   The Clwydian Hills

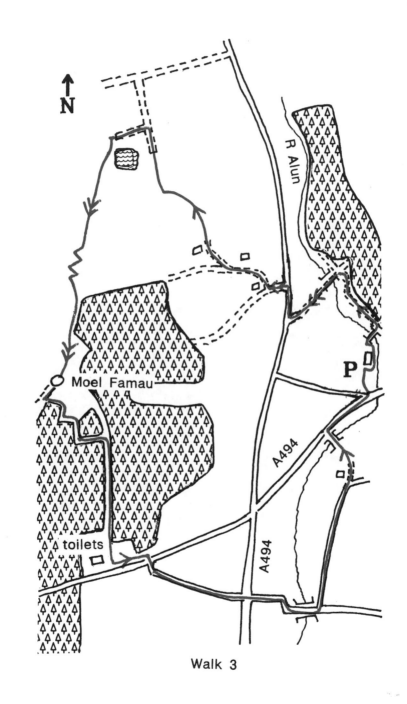

N

R Alun

P

Moel Famau

A494

A494

toilets

Walk 3

THE CLWYDIAN RANGE

3.   Moel Famau and Ffrith Mountain

Ordnance Survey Map No: 116
Distance from city centre: 57.5km/35ml
Walking distance: 13km/8ml
Amount of climbing: 512km/1690ft
A varied walk through woods and over moorland with splendid views of Snowdonia and the Lancashire coast.

Park at the Country Park Centre, Loggerheads. SD198626. To get there take Wallasey tunnel, M53 to J5 and A550/A494 to Mold and Loggerheads. Carpark on right at foot of hill.

Cross R. Alun which is on far side of the Information Centre and turn left to follow river on left. Pass boarding kennels and a white gate, beyond which take small path on left down to a bridge. Cross and follow track up to lane. Turn right and after 400m/0.25ml go up bridleway on left leaving it by a bungalow for another bridleway on right after 400m/0.25ml.

Follow this bridleway, at times less distinct, through numerous gates taking right-hand fork at junction by brick ruins in trees and through farmyard beyond. Soon path drops; at bottom go left between hedges on bridleway, through gate and uphill SW with reservoir on left and under trees. At open ground path zigzags steeply to corner of plantation and then to summit of Moel

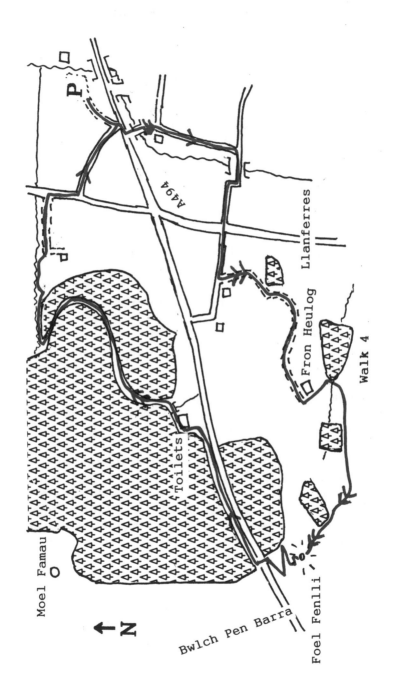

Famau. Views are well marked on four panorama boards.

Descend by the very broad track SSW, but leave this after 400m/0.25ml at a stile on left. Blue waymarkers show route down. It follows the edge of the forest on right; goes downhill; through a firebreak on the right; turns left and then right at a forest road down to a carpark (toilets on right). Turn left through carpark and walk through trees beyond for 350m/0.2ml parallel to road, watching for small lane going off to right.

Cross road and go down this lane to junction with A494. Cross and continue on lane, cross river and take first lane on left. When this turns sharp right at top of hill, keep ahead on bridleway down to main road, cross and turn right back to carpark.

This walk may be shortened by turning left downhill by the plantation at the top of the zigzags. This leads back to the brick ruins where you turn right. Save 1.5km/0.8ml.

4.   Foel Fenlli

Ordnance Survey Map No: 116
Distance from city centre: 57.5km/35ml
Walking distance: 13km/8ml
Amount of climbing: 440km/1452ft

Another lovely walk in the Clwydian Hills, this time visiting the summit of an iron-age hill fort.

Park at the Country Park Centre, Loggerheads. SD198626. To get there take the Wallasey tunnel, M53 to J5 and A550/A494 to Mold and Loggerheads. Carpark on right at foot of hill.

From carpark return to main road, cross and turn right. After 200m/220yd turn left, cross bridge and follow track uphill. Continue ahead when track is metalled and go downhill. Turn right, cross river and after reaching main road cross again to continue on lane on far side. After 0.9km/0.5ml turn left through a gate up track just before white cottage. Keep on this track which contours to just above farm of Bron Heulog,

29

making sure that when wooden sheep-dips are reached you keep ahead and turn sharp left at far end and do not go through gate on left before them.

With farm on left, pass through two gates close together and another left, going downhill to top of small wood. Cross stream and then stile in wall ahead. Turn right and follow Offa's Dyke signs over stiles uphill with wall and then wood on right. Path goes left of another wood and then steeply uphill. When wooden post indicates that Offa's Dyke path goes left, keep straight ahead uphill for summit. From summit cairn take middle track ahead and when rampart is reached turn left for 20m/22yd and then right to pick up very steep zigzag track down to Bwlch Pen Barra.

Turn right, cross cattle grid and go up left on to track which goes downhill with road on right. After 1.1km/0.5ml track joins road and just ahead are public toilets. Go left of these, cross small bridge, turn left and take forestry road through gate (signposted for mountain bikes – "approved forest road only"). Do not take any of the tracks on left, but keep on this track, at first uphill, for 2.5km/1.5ml. Track curves right back on itself and as it drops look for small parallel path below at forest edge.

Track turns sharply right and the small path joins it. Turn right along path, now going NE instead of SW. After 0.5km/0.2ml cross stile on left and turn right at signpost to Loggerheads. This path leads to a small lane. Turn right and take left fork on lane which leads down to main road and carpark.

This walk can be shortened by continuing down lane past public toilets and turning left at main road. Save 2.5km/1.25ml.

Walk 3   Moel Famau

Walk 12   Pen yr Helgi Ddu and Craig yr Ysfa from the east

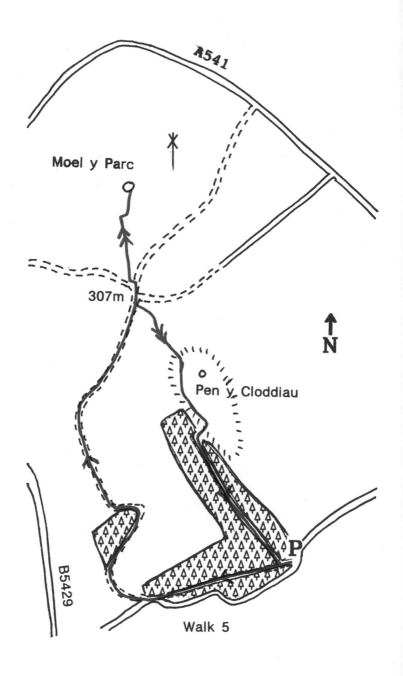

A541

Moel y Parc

307m

Pen y Cloddiau

N

B5429

P

Walk 5

5.   *Penycloddiau and Moel y Parc*

Ordnance Survey Map No: 116
Distance from city centre: 67km/40ml
Walking distance: 10.8km/6.5ml
Amount of climbing: 305m/1000ft

A gentle walk through woodland and along an ancient trackway, with a visit to a hill fort.

Park at a small Forestry Commission carpark on minor road. SJ139668. To get there take the Wallasey tunnel, M53 to J5 and A550/A494 to Mold. Turn right on A541 towards Denbigh and after 9.6km/6ml, turn left to Nannerch, but before entering village take minor road left to Llandyrnog. Parking at top of pass right.

Go through gate into forest. There are four tracks. Follow the track on the extreme left down to a lane which is taken for a few yards before track continues ahead in same direction. Track rises gently and contours for 3.2km/2ml to a pass at 307m/1013ft.

Go through gate (Offa's Dyke signs–white acorn) and ahead for 20m/22yd to cross stile on left. Go uphill with fence on right until triangulation pillar comes into view. Cross at any convenient point and go to summit of Moel y Parc for extensive views N along coast and W towards Snowdonia.

Retrace steps to gate and turn left (SE). Follow Offa's Dyke signs up and over the top of the hill fort of Penycloddiau and down through the left-hand edge of the forest back to the carpark.

This walk may be shortened by omitting the climb to the top of Moel y Parc and turning right at the gate on meeting the Offa's Dyke path. Save 3km/1.8ml.

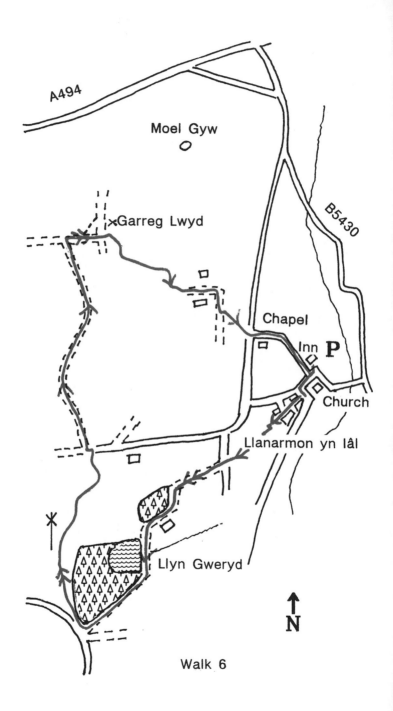

A494

Moel Gyw

Garreg Lwyd

B5430

Chapel

Inn **P**

Church

Llanarmon yn Iâl

Llyn Gweryd

N

Walk 6

6. Llyn Gweryd

Ordnance Survey Map No: 116
Distance from city centre: 53km/33ml
Walking distance: 10km/6.25ml
Amount of climbing: 300m/1000ft

A walk in tranquil countryside which takes in part of Offa's Dyke path and has the advantage of being superbly signposted. Clwyd C.C. and its countryside staff deserve a special award from the Ramblers' Association.

Park in the village of Llanarmon yn iâl by the Raven Inn. SJ191562. To get there take the Wallasey tunnel, M53 to J5 and A550/A494 to Mold and then towards Ruthin. Turn left to Llanarmon on B5430 and after 3.3km/2ml go right on B5431. Parking is on right.

From the inn turn right and follow lane as it turns left to church and go right on signposted footpath opposite church. Follow path through housing until it exits on far right into field. Cross stile on left, turn right and continue over stiles to lane. Cross and go up bridleway ahead, keeping on this lane as it curves left and right past fly fishery, deer compound, Llyn Gweryd on right, felled woods and newly planted trees, to a lane.

Turn right and follow the white acorns marking Offa's Dyke Long Distance Footpath (LDP). This leads up past a transmitter, and down a slope, uphill to a fence, right and then left over a stile. The path contours round the hill and drops down to a lane at a col. Half left the LDP continues in the same direction, contouring until another track is met above some sheep-folds where it turns sharp right uphill to a col. Continue on track to the left of two gates just after OD path goes left.

A few metres on left is Garreg Llwyd, the Grey Stone, which marks the meeting point of three parishes, but our route is half-right to a concrete ladder stile on the near skyline. From this stile go right to gate and stile and continue E along ridge with wall on left. Turn right at cross wall and left over stile. A clear

*Walks 7, 9, 10 and 11   Snowdon, Tryfan, the Glyders and
Y Garn*

path leads down to other stiles and on to a track by
converted farm buildings. Turn left and follow track
past pond on left, going left on next stile, across field
to lane by chapel. Continue on lane ahead with chapel
on right and it will bring you directly back to the
Raven.

It is possible to shorten this walk by turning downhill
on the lane at the col after the transmitter. Save 1.5km/
1ml.

Walk 3   Moel Famau

Walk 13   Cregiau Gleision

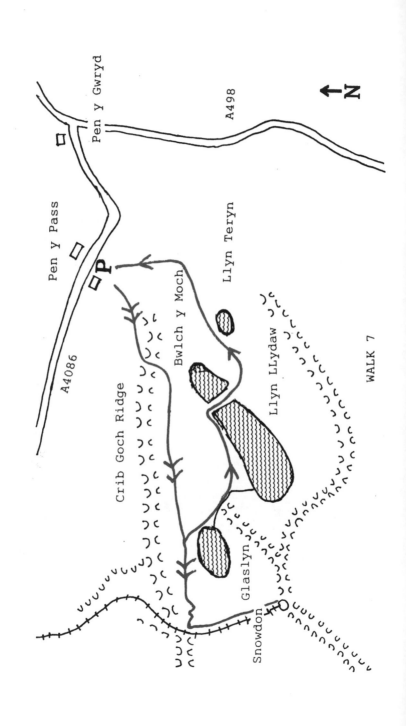

Pen y Gwryd

A498

N

Pen y Pass

P

A4086

Bwlch y Moch

Llyn Teryn

Crib Goch Ridge

Llyn Llydaw

WALK 7

Glaslyn

Snowdon

SNOWDONIA AND NORTH WALES

7. *Snowdon by the Pyg and Miners' Tracks*

Ordnance Survey Map No: 115 or OL No 17
Distance from city centre: 135km/84ml
Walking distance: 12km/7.5ml
Amount of climbing: 726m/2400ft

Yr Wyddfa, although climbed by thousands annu-
ally, is not a mountain to be taken lightly, especially
in winter conditions. This walk combines two of the
many exhilarating routes to the summit of the highest
mountain in Wales.

Park at Pen y Pass opposite the Youth Hostel.
SH647556. To get there take Wallasey tunnel, M53
to J5, A550/A494 to Ewloe and A55 to Llandudno
Junction; A470 to Betws y Coed; A5 to Capel Curig
and A4086 to Pen y Pass.

When facing S, the Pyg Track is the wide stony path
leading from the right of the carpark. Take this track
and after 2km/1.25ml take fork left at Bwlch y Moch.
Above right is Crib Goch ridge and below, first Llyn
Llydaw and then Glaslyn. Note where Miners' Track
joins from left (for the descent). Route is now steeper
but keeps to the famous zigzags until mountain railway
is reached. Turn left for summit.

Descend as far as junction with Miners' Track and

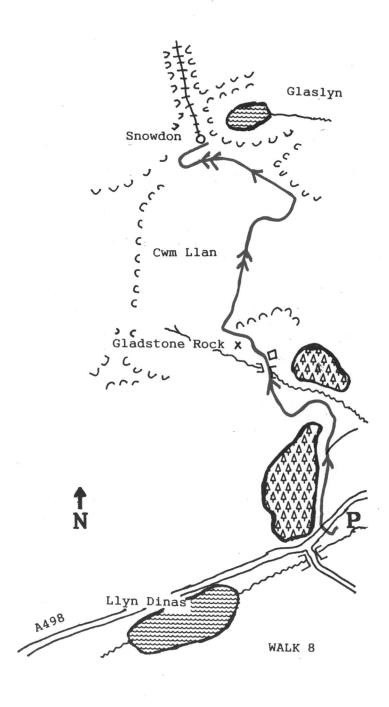

Glaslyn

Snowdon

Cwm Llan

Gladstone Rock ✗

N

P.

Llyn Dinas

A498

WALK 8

fork right. Follow this obvious track down, passing ruins of miners' barracks and crossing Llyn Llydaw by causeway en route to carpark.

It is not possible to shorten this walk if the summit is to be visited. If a shorter walk is desired then turn left on reaching the Miners' Track. Save 3km/1.75ml.

8.   Snowdon by the Watkin Path

Ordnance Survey Map No: 115 or OL No 17
Distance from city centre: 138km/86ml
Walking distance: 13km/8ml
Amount of climbing: 1025m/3383ft

Few mountain tracks can have had an official opening, as this path did. Constructed by Sir Edward Watkin and opened by Gladstone on 13 September 1892, it provides a straightforward and agreeable ascent which can be combined with one of the routes in walk 7 if transport at the end is available.

Park off the A498 between the two lakes, Gwynant and Dinas. SH628507. To get there take the Wallasey tunnel, M53 to J5, A550/A494 to Ewloe, A55 to Llandudno Junction, A470 to Betws y Coed, A5 to Capel Curig, A4086 to Pen y Gwryd and the A498 signposted Beddgelert. Carpark on left.

Cross the road, turn left and go up the lane to the right of the shops opposite, following the edge of the wood. The track curves around the little rocky peak of Castell and after passing waterfalls on right, levels out. Cross the stream to keep right in Cwm Llan and climb to Bwlch y Saethau. The track now climbs steeply over scree to the left as far as the ridge. Turn right for the summit. Return by outward route.

It is not possible to shorten this route if the summit is to be visited, but Cwm Llan and Bwlch y Saethau are good objectives in themselves. Save 9km/2.5ml and 3km/1.8ml respectively.

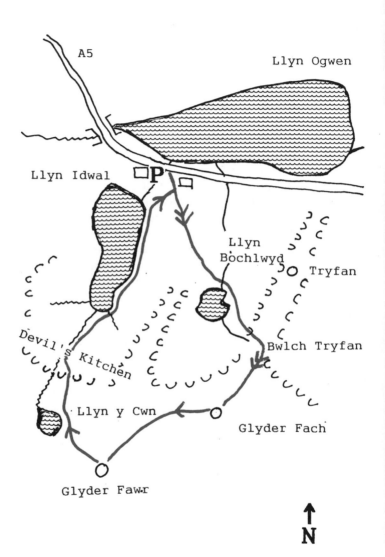

WALK 9

9. The Glyders

Ordnance Survey Map No: 115 or OL No 17
Distance from city centre: 133km/83ml
Walking distance: 8km/5ml
Amount of climbing: 774m/2554ft

A spectacular landscape to walk in with all the feel of high mountains. Not for the inexperienced except in good weather and in summer.

Park off the A5 at the W end of Llyn Ogwen near the Youth Hostel. SH649604. (Other parking on A5 to E.) To get there take the Wallasey tunnel, M53 to J5, A550/A494 to Ewloe, A55 to Llandudno Junction, A470 to Betws y Coed and A5 to Llyn Ogwen.

The path to Llyn Idwal starts from the carpark near the refreshment kiosk. Where this well-engineered path bends right keep ahead on a less distinct path which goes to the right of waterfalls. Cross stream at outlet and continue with Llyn Bochlwyd on right to Bwlch Tryfan, a col.

Cross ladder stile and turn up right, either scrambling up ridge or up scree below on its left. On summit plateau follow a faint cairned path SW to the so-called Cantilever, the summit of Glyder Fach, continuing to the Castle of the Winds and the summit of Glyder Fawr.

From the summit go W for 100m/110yd and then NW down a scree slope to Llyn y Cwn. Here turn right (NE) on a track, boggy at first, then entering a rocky depression which leads below the cleft of the Devil's Kitchen. The descent is now steep and rocky as far as Llyn Idwal. There are good paths on both sides of the lake which meet at the N end and join the outward route.

There is no practicable way of shortening this route as the alternatives (Y Gribin or Cwm Bochlwyd) are over more difficult ground.

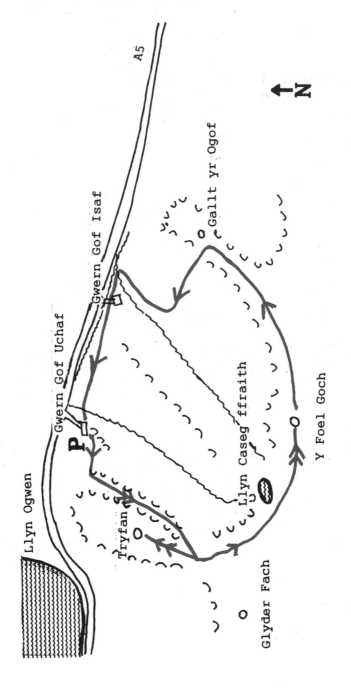

WALK 10

N

A5

Llyn Ogwen

Gwern Gof Uchaf

Gwern Gof Isaf

P

Gallt yr Ogof

Tryfan

Llyn Caseg ffraith

Y Foel Goch

Glyder Fach

10. Tryfan

Ordnance Survey Map No: 115 or OL No 17
Distance from city centre: 130km/81ml
Walking distance: 9km/5.6ml
Amount of climbing: 750m/2480ft

One of the finest mountain summits in Britain, Tryfan offers many ways of ascent, none less than interesting and many of them difficult rock climbs. The highest point demands some nerve to attain.

Park (fee) at Gwern Gof Uchaf, a farm off the A5. SH673604. To get there take the Wallasey tunnel, M53 to J5, A550/A494 to Ewloe, A55 to Llandudno Junction, A470 to Betws y Coed and A5 to Ogwen. Farm on left.

Go over a ladder stile to left of farm and walk SW to the foot of the outcrop of Tryfan Bach. Take a path right, first across marsh aiming for the Heather Terrace which is clearly seen crossing the face of Tryfan below the rock faces. Care is needed to find the start of the terrace but once on it turn left and go straight up with no problems to the col to the S of Tryfan. Here, climb the ladder stile and turn right up to the summit.

Begin the descent by going back to the col and over the stile. From here go S and then SW, contouring above Cwm Tryfan, first to Llyn Caseg Fraith and then W to Y Foel Goch. Continue now NE to Gallt yr Ogof. After 600m/0.33ml turn sharply left down into Cwm Gwern Gof as the route along the ridge leads only to cliffs. Follow the stream down to a gate on a bridleway just to the E of Gwern gof Isaf farm. Turn left and return to Gwern gof Uchaf.

This walk may be shortened by turning N just before Llyn Caseg Fraith and following a track direct to the carpark. Save 2km/1.25ml.

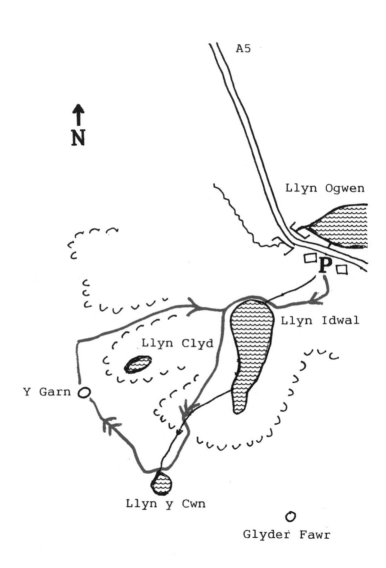

WALK 11

11. Y Garn

Ordnance Survey Map No: 115 or OL No 17
Distance from city centre: 133km/83ml
Walking distance: 8km/5ml
Amount of climbing: 650m/2135ft

Although not as frequently climbed as Tryfan or the Glyders, Y Garn's isolation makes it a splendid viewpoint in all directions.

Park off the A5 at the W end of Llyn Ogwen near the Youth Hostel. SH649604. (Other parking on A5 to E.) To get there take the Wallasey tunnel, M53 to J5, A550/A494 to Ewloe, A55 to Llandudno Junction, A470 to Betws y Coed and A5 to Ogwen.

Take the path to Llyn Idwal near the refreshment kiosk and follow it all the way to an iron gate by the lake. Go through the gate and follow the track to W of Llyn Idwal and up the steep track below the Devil's Kitchen to Llyn y Cwn. At the outlet to the lake take the track N to the summit of Y Garn.

The descent is well trodden but requires some care to find. Follow the rim of the cliffs NW until meeting a ridge going NE after 400m/0.25ml. Follow the track as it curves mostly just to the right of this ridge and down to the N end of Llyn Idwal to meet the outward path.

It is not possible to shorten this walk although a stroll around Cwm Idwal is recommended for a half day or in bad weather.

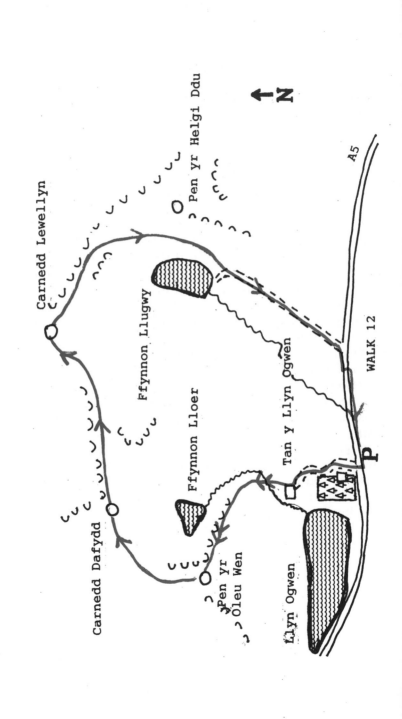

Carnedd Lewellyn

Pen yr Helgi Ddu

N

A5

Ffynnon Llugwy

Ffynnon Lloer

Tan y Llyn Ogwen

WALK 12

Carnedd Dafydd

Pen yr
Oleu Wen

P

Llyn Ogwen

12. *Pen yr Oleu Wen and the Carneddau*

Ordnance Survey Map No: 115 or OL Nos 16 and 17
Distance from city centre: 131km/82ml
Walking distance: 16km/10ml
Amount of climbing: 1082m/3570ft

This walk begins with a very hard climb but remains at 3000ft for several miles, bringing a real sense of isolation between the two Carneddau.

Park off the A5 opposite the little conifer wood at the E end of Llyn Ogwen. SH668605. Other parking on A5 nearby. To get there take the Wallasey tunnel, M53 to J5, A550/A494 to Ewloe, A55 to Llandudno Junction, A470 to Betws y Coed and A5 to Ogwen.

To the right of the wood a track leads N to the farm of Tan y Llyn Ogwen, over a ladder stile, crosses the Afon Loer and keeps to its left to a second stile. From this point go E to the ridge on left which, after some easy scrambling, leads to the summit of Pen yr Oleu Wen. The main path goes N and then NE to Carnedd Dafydd and then E along the top of the cliffs of Ysgolion Duon. At a col the route goes NE to Carnedd Llewelyn.

Just S of the summit the path to Craig yr Ysfa is indicated by a cairn. Go E and then SE to a col between Craig yr Ysfa and Pen yr Helgi Ddu and directly N of Ffynnon Llugwy. Instead of climbing, take the track down to the E of the lake and follow the access road SW to the A5. Turn right and after 250m/0.2ml cross road to a bridge over stream to pick up bridleway going W back to carpark.

The walk may be shortened by going SE after Ysgolion Duon to Craig Llugwy and then S to the farm of Glan Llugwy and following the farm road back to A5, saving 5km/3ml. The ground is very rough and steep, however, and it is not recommended.

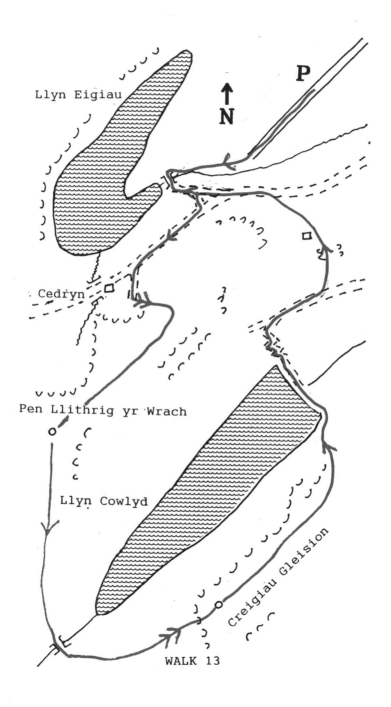

Llyn Eigiau

N

P

Cedryn

Pen Llithrig yr Wrach

Llyn Cowlyd

Creigiau Gleision

WALK 13

13. Pen Llithrig y Wrach and Creigiau Gleision

Ordnance Survey Map No: 115 or OL No 16
Distance from city centre: 117km/73ml
Walking distance: 16km/10ml
Amount of climbing: 912m/3010ft

A good walk for summer bank-holidays. Because of its relative inaccessibility and lack of famous names, this side of Snowdonia is still less popular.

Park at end of road from Tal y Bont. SH732663. To get there take Wallasey tunnel, M53 to J5, A550/A494 to Ewloe, A55 to Llandudno Junction and A470 to Betws y Coed as far as Tal y Cafn. Here turn right to cross R. Conwy and at crossroads in Ty'n y Groes turn left on B5106. Immediately after crossing river in Talybont turn right up small lane and drive to carpark at end.

Follow track SW past Llyn Eigiau. At 400m/0.25ml before Cedryn (a small cottage) a grassy track leads to a ruin above and after a few yards crosses a fence. Go uphill with fence on left to its corner. A grassy rake can be seen above leading up to right. Follow this and then an intermittent track to a stream which leads almost to the ridge. From here it is a straightforward walk SW to the summit of Pen Llithrig yr Wrach. In descending, avoid cliffs E by taking a line S along the top of crags and making for footbridge in valley.

Cross this and climb NNE to summit of Creigiau Gleision then along ridge to N summit from which a fence leads down to Llyn Cowlyd. Cross below dam and go up zigzag track opposite to join another track. Turn right and after 300m/0.2ml turn left at some sheepfolds (Garreg Wen) up a shallow valley. When the track is more obvious there is a white waymark. Go over shoulder of hill, past a deserted farm to a large track. Turn left to join outward route by Llyn Eigiau. Turn right back to carpark.

This walk can be shortened by omitting the climb to Creigiau Gleision and going NW along the N shore of Llyn Cowlyd. The distance saved is insignificant but the route is quicker and avoids 263m/870ft of climbing.

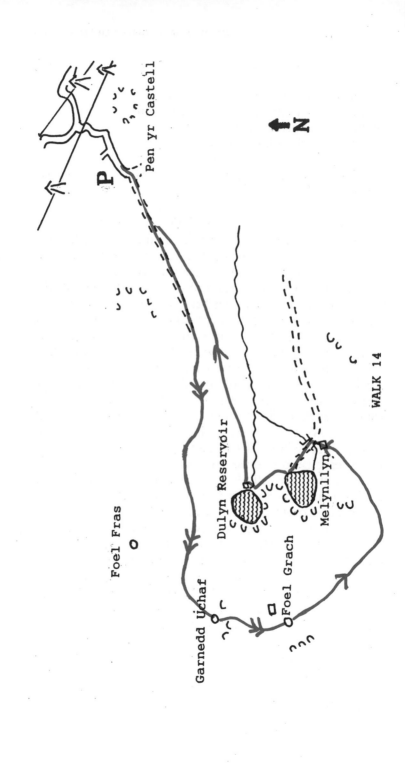

N

Pen yr Castell

P

Foel Fras

Garnedd Uchaf

Dulyn Reservoir

Foel Grach

Melynllyn

WALK 14

14. *Foel Grach*

Ordnance Survey Map No: 115 or OL 16
Distance from city centre: 101km/63ml
Walking distance: 16km/10ml
Amount of climbing: 662m/2185ft

Another walk on the less-frequented side of the Carneddau, at times on engineered tracks, but often on grassy slopes. Navigation on top can be difficult in bad weather.

Park at the side of the lane at Bwlch y Gaer. SH743692. To get there take the Wallasey tunnel, M53 to J5, A550/494 to Ewloe, A55 to Llandudno Junction and A470 towards Betws y Coed as far as Tal y Cafn. Here turn right to cross the R. Conwy and at the crossroads in Ty'n y Groes turn left on the B5106. Just before the inn in Tal y Bont take the lane on right to Llanbedr y Cennin. Ignore the turning right by the chapel and continue up a very steep and narrow lane. After a ferocious left bend take an even smaller lane on left in the middle of a wide right curve and pass beneath power lines. After 1km/0.7ml the end of the lane is reached. Park on left.

Walk SW along the stony track with a wall on the left at first. After 2km/1.25ml the track gives way to grass and there is a steady climb W on the S flank of Foel Fras to the ridge. Turn S to reach the mountain shelter on the summit of Foel Grach.

Descend by taking the path SE but after 1km/0.6ml bear E and then NE on a grassy ridge ending at spot height 735m/2400ft. To the E and NE are crags but by turning N a track below can be reached. Turn left on the track, taking a short-cut by a building across to the N outlet of Melynllyn where a less-defined path hugs the base of some cliffs to the Dulyn Reservoir. Turn right on to another track which leads directly back to the carpark.

It is not practicable to shorten this route.

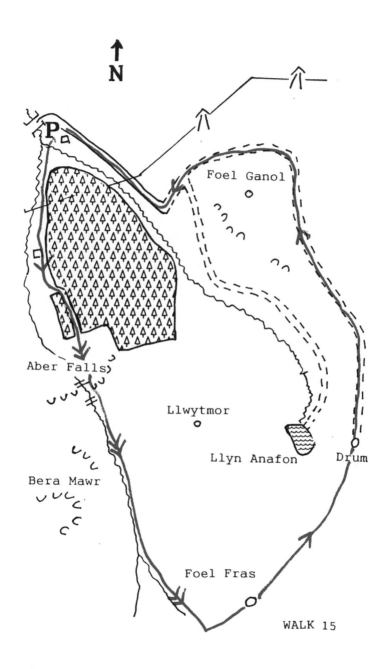

N

P

Foel Ganol

Aber Falls

Llwytmor

Llyn Anafon

Drum

Bera Mawr

Foel Fras

WALK 15

15. Drum and Foel Fras

Ordnance Survey Map No: 115 or OL Nos 16 and 17
Distance from city centre: 109km/68ml
Walking distance: 16km/10ml
Amount of climbing: 933m/3079ft

A walk which includes one of the finest waterfalls in Wales and a 3000ft peak in the relative solitude of the Carneddau.

Park in Forestry Commission carpark SE of Aber village. SH664719. To get there take the Wallasey tunnel, M53 to J5, A550/A494 to Ewloe and A55 to Aber. At Aber turn left on a minor road leading through village to carpark.

Follow the E bank of the river upstream, under power lines and take a fork left just before a cottage, keeping to the right-hand edge of the wood. A stile on left leads into the wood and a path runs S through the wood and out again on to scree near the waterfall. Cross the scree and follow the stream on a high-level path on its E bank all the way to its source, continuing in the same direction (SE) to the col between Garnedd Uchaf and Foel Fras. Turn left and go NE to Foel Fras. From here a wall and then a fence lead to Drum.

From Drum a rough track goes N and then NW round the N shoulder of Foel Ganol ending at the minor road which leads down to the carpark.

To shorten the walk descend from the col between Foel Fras and Drum to a track which leads from Llyn Anafon to the road. The descent is, however, steep and treacherous and hardly worth the saving of 1.5km/1ml.

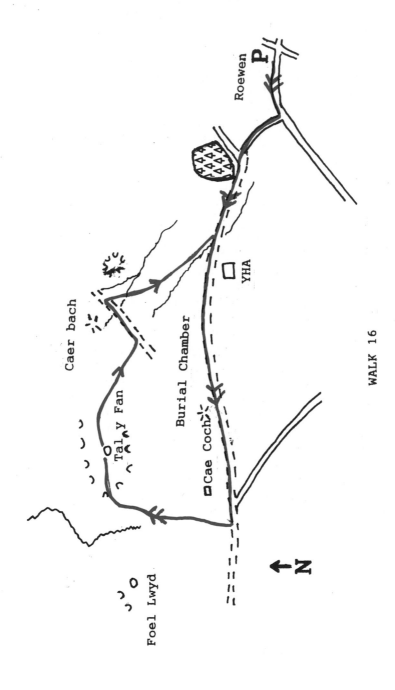

Roewen

P

Caer bach

Tal y Fan

Burial Chamber

YHA

Cae Coch

Foel Lwyd

N

WALK 16

16. Tal y Fan

Ordnance Survey Map No: 115 or OL No 16
Distance from city centre: 104km/65ml
Walking distance: 9.0km/5.5ml
Amount of climbing: 616m/2033ft

An easy walk in charming surroundings, affording beautiful views and passing some interesting antiquities.

Park at E end of Roewen village. SH760720. To get there take the Wallasey tunnel, M53 to J5, A550/A494 to Ewloe, A55 to Llandudno Junction and A47 towards Betws y Coed as far as Tal y Cafn. Here turn right to cross the R. Conwy. At the crossroads in Ty'n y Groes turn left and take the first right to Roewen. Park on right before entering village.

Go W through the village, turning right at a junction and continuing up a track (Roman road) past the Youth Hostel on to a rough track, noting the burial chamber on right. Join a metalled lane and after 70m/78yd cross the wall on right by a ladder stile and follow white marker posts uphill. Cross wall on ridge and follow it up right to summit of Tal y Fan.

Follow ridge ENE and then SE with wall on right. Note that, as on the ascent, there are many small crags but that they are more difficult to spot going downhill. All can be easily avoided.

When ground levels out turn left at iron gate in wall with a low wall on right for 600m/0.4ml. Aim for a rocky outcrop half-right. At a distinct gap in the low wall a ladder stile can be seen on right over another wall. Cross this and go SE until meeting a stream with a wall beyond on the other side of this large field. Follow stream down to stile on road below Youth Hostel. Turn left back to village.

It is not practicable to shorten this walk.

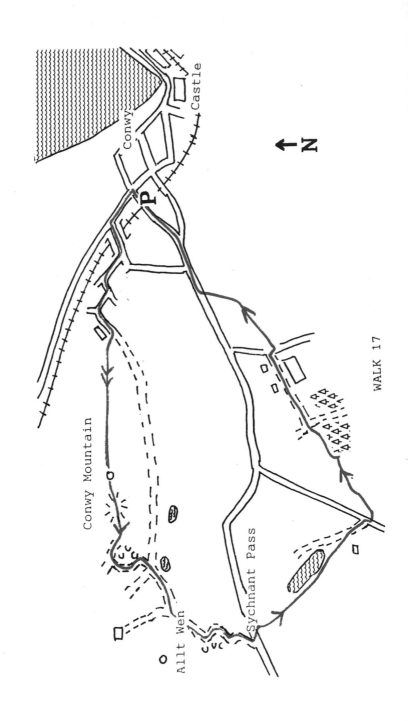

Castle

Conwy

P

Conwy Mountain

Allt Wen

Sychnant Pass

N

WALK 17

17. Conwy Mountain

Ordnance Survey Map No: 115 or OL No 16
Distance from city centre: 96km/60ml
Walking distance: 8km/5.25ml
Amount of climbing: 245m/809ft

An easy climb from Conwy affords splendid sea and mountain views and can be combined in a day with a visit to the town itself.

Park in Mount Pleasant. SH779775. To get there take the Wallasey tunnel, M53 to J5, A550/A494 to Ewloe and A55 to Conwy. Follow one-way system through town, turning sharp left after passing through gap in town walls. Other parking in town but walk starts at this point.

Walk back to where road passes through wall and turn left (NW). Cross railway on left and then turn right with railway on right. Turn right (Mountain Road) just after the road curves left and follow it left at sign "To Mountain Road". At far end of terrace of houses on right follow footpath sign up narrow track to right.

When this track forks near ridge, turn right and then left after 50m/55yd and keep to highest ground to summit. Continue W over ruins of hill fort and descend towards rocky knoll. The whole area is a maze of tracks but keep to the most obvious to the right of the rocky knoll and round to the other side. Continue in the same direction over a crossing track with a pond on left. Top a small rise and descend to a rough farm track. Turn left and follow it as it curves round to the tarmac road at the top of the Sychnant Pass.

Cross road to gate on far side and walk with wall on left until reaching a ladder stile. Cross and pass small lake left before joining a stony track. On reaching a stone wall on the right follow it downhill to road. Turn right and after 100m/110yd go through kissing gate on left, immediately before a house. Walk between fences through two more kissing gates and turn left to cross a drive and go through a gate.

Continue through fields keeping close to wood on

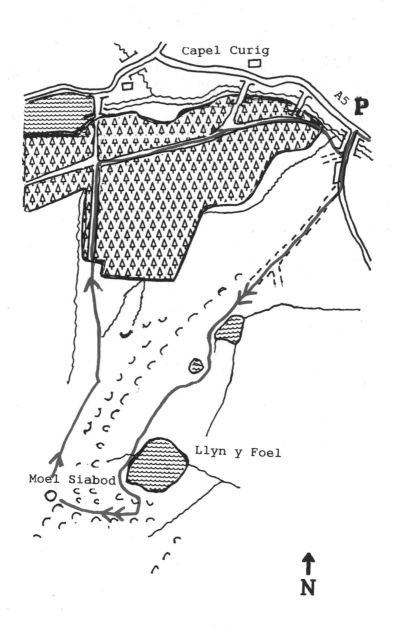

Capel Curig

A5 P

Llyn y Foel

Moel Siabod

N

WALK 18

hill on right (superb primroses in season). Turn right on drive which is followed between buildings to lane. Turn right and then left through kissing gate to cross fields. In last field go left to follow field edge to road. Turn right to return to Conwy.

This walk could be shortened by walking back to Conwy directly from the top of the Sychnant Pass but the distance saved is insignificant.

18. Moel Siabod

Ordnance Survey Map No: 115 or OL No 16
Distance from city centre: 125km/78ml
Walking distance: 9.6km/6ml
Amount of climbing: 4212m/1390ft

A fine climb up a mountain of distinction with some scrambling.

Park in a large lay-by N side of A5 150m/165yd E of Pont Cyfing. SH736571. To get there take the Wallasey tunnel, M53 to J5, A550/A494 to Ewloe, A55 to Llandudno Junction, A470 to Betws y Coed and A5 to Capel Curig. Park before reaching main village.

Cross Pont Cyfing, which is on S side of A5. Bear right at second fork, taking the old quarry road SW to the right of a small lake and then left of a water-filled quarry. Signposts lead to the right of Llyn y Foel. Climb right up the edge of the E ridge to the summit.

The way down is by the NE ridge at first but after 700m/2300ft turn N and aim roughly for the E end of the lake ahead (Llynnau Mymbyr). The indistinct path becomes clearer and is cairned to a ladder stile. Cross and continue down into the forest to a forest road. Turn right and follow this road until another forest road joins from the left. After 55m/60yd fork right again on a riverside path.

You can turn left over a footbridge to Cobden's Hotel on the A5 and turn right to the lay-by but to avoid the traffic it is better to continue on the riverside path to Pont Cyfing.

It is not possible to shorten this walk.

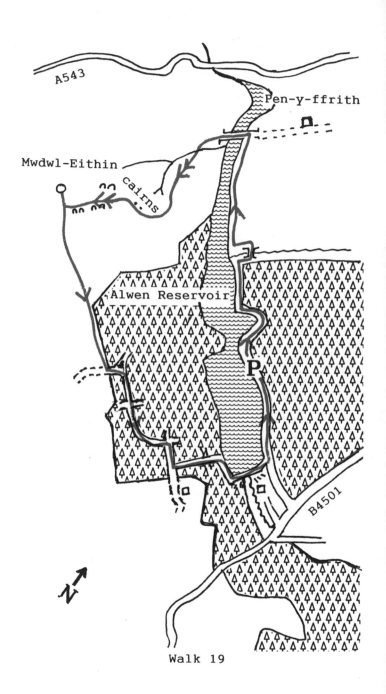

A543

Pen-y-ffrith

Mwdwl-Eithin

cairns

Alwen Reservoir

P

B4501

Walk 19

N

19. Hiraethog-Mynydd Mwdwl-Eithin

Ordnance Survey Map No: 116
Distance from city centre: 85km/53ml
Walking distance: 14km/8.75ml
Amount of climbing: 202m/667ft

The vast Hiraethog area is boggy, heather-covered and virtually trackless, and for these reasons is likely to be one of the few places in North Wales where you will meet no other walker. Although this walk touches only the fringes, you are urged not to go alone or when visibility is poor. Such tracks as exist are ill-defined and difficult to follow and you need to be able to keep your objective in view.

Park in the Forestry Commission carpark on the NE bank of Alwen Reservoir. SH948537. To get there take the Wallasey tunnel, M53 to J5 and A550/A494 to Mold and Ruthin. Follow signs for Corwen and Bala (A494) and on outskirts of Ruthin keep straight ahead on B5105 to Cerrigydrudion instead of turning left to Bala. In Cerrigydrudion turn right on B4501, following tourist signs to Llyn Brenig Visitor Centre. Road drops to cross river and then climbs again. Take forest road left signposted for fishing and picnics. Pass dam and drive as far as you can on this road to carpark by lakeside on left.

From carpark take lakeside path NW. At end of large bay, after crossing stream go up to right to forest edge to drier ground. At end of forest turn right and cross bridge. *There is no access across fence to right of way shown on map and path itself has been lost in recent re-planting*. Turn left and return to water's edge, where after an initial boggy patch there is a well-trodden path. Cross footbridge and on far side go up to sheepfold before crossing stream on left.

Path goes SSW and passes through gap in ruined fence. After a few paces summit can be seen and path heads towards it, before turning SE to gate on skyline on left. The fence here leads to within a few metres of summit, but there is no path and the terrain is desperately difficult. The faint path that follows winds around to take advantage of easier ground, avoiding heather.

Continue to top of little rise ahead. Path goes S but gradually swings round SW heading for summit.

Watch for small cairn on right of path and go up to right on grass strip. On reaching large grass area, cross, going W. Again, look for small cairn. Once over brow, first the summit and then an outcrop of rock with sheepfold can be seen. This lies to right of path but is an excellent place for lunch. Ahead two more small outcrops are visible and path goes over top of both before reaching broad swathe cut through heather which leads to small pass. Turn right to go up to summit. There is no path but it is a short walk to the summit and there is a well-built shelter near TP.

There is no right of way to and from the summit but agents for the landowners have indicated that if users of this book behave responsibly and cause no damage, then it is unlikely that any objection will be made to their presence.

Walk 19   Alwen Reservoir and Mwdwl Eithin

Walk 19   Alwen Reservoir

From summit descend to pass again and continue SE (no path) making for corner of plantation. On reaching forest, walk with trees and fence on left until stone wall appears behind fence where faint track enters plantation from right. Enter forest, negotiating windfallen trees. Cross stream and with stream on right go down to forest road. Turn right.

Keep ahead at crossroads. Road swings left to second crossroads. Turn right to gate at forest edge. Before gate turn left with wall on right. Keep ahead when wall ends and at cross paths. Cross stream, turn right and continue with stream on right to forest road. Cross and continue with stream now on left to edge of reservoir. Turn right, cross dam and turn left on far bank to reach carpark.

It is not practicable to shorten this walk.

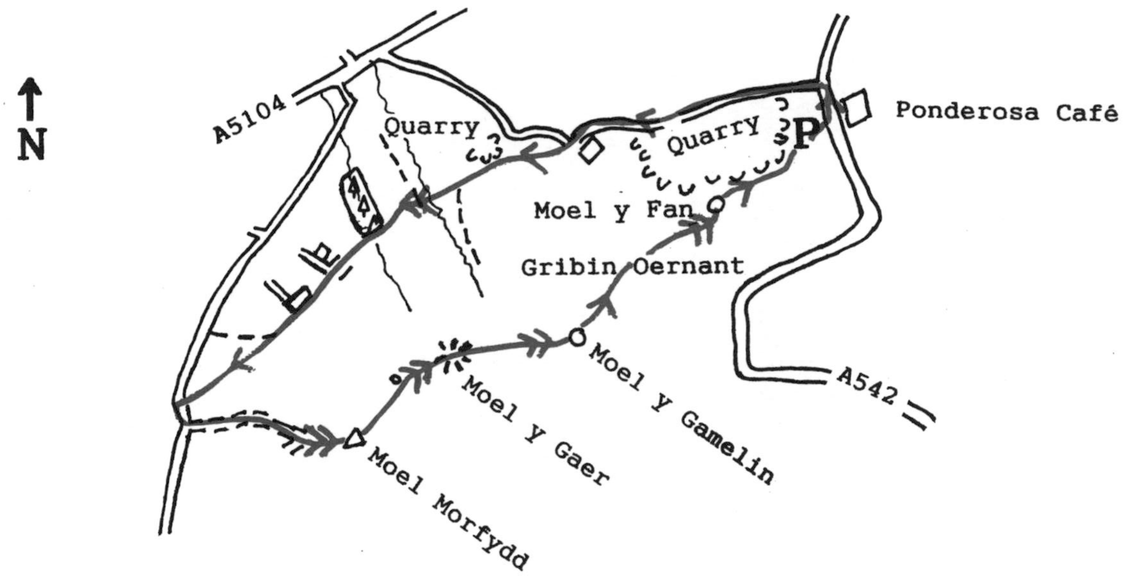

Ponderosa Café

A542

Quarry

P

Moel y Fan

Gribin Oernant

Moel y Gamelin

Moel y Gaer

Quarry

Moel Morfydd

A5104

N

Walk 20

20. Llantisilio Mountain

Ordnance Survey Map No: 116
Distance from city centre: 87km/34ml
Walking distance: 11.5km/7ml
Amount of climbing: 700m/2310ft

This walk makes use of a bridleway which is on the map and on the ground but which is completely without waymarking. There are no stiles and the gates are wired up to keep out motor-cyclists. However, farmers I have spoken to on the route are well disposed towards walkers and there are no difficulties in crossing the obstacles. It's all legal and provides good views of Snowdonia and Llangollen.

Park on the W side of A542 opposite Ponderosa Cafe. SJ192481. To get there take the Wallasey tunnel, M53 to J5 and A550/A494 to junction with A55. Take A55 (Wrexham) turning-off at next exit on to A550 (Wrexham) and then A5104 (Corwen). After Pen y Stryt turn left at roundabout on to A542 (Llangollen). Parking on right at top of hill opposite cafe.

From carpark turn left (N) and after 50m/55yd go left down small lane which runs along edge of quarry on left. After 2km/1.25ml there is a cottage to left on bend in road. Go up grassy slope starting by gate on left and cross fence just above lane. Bridleway is visible as level strip on hillside due W. Pass above quarry on right and cross fence; path, now clear through heather, contours with stone wall on right. Keep close to broken wall and fence when it drops down to stream. Go *beneath* anti-motor-cyclist fence and climb hillside on far bank on track slanting half-right. Track passes two more gates before dropping downhill and turning sharp right. At this point do not go right but cross old gate in front to keep in same direction; bridleway soon becomes clear again.

Cross two small streams and pass above farm on right, close to corrugated iron barn, with fence on right again. Cross gate, keep line of trees on right and cross another gate. Do not follow fence on right down to

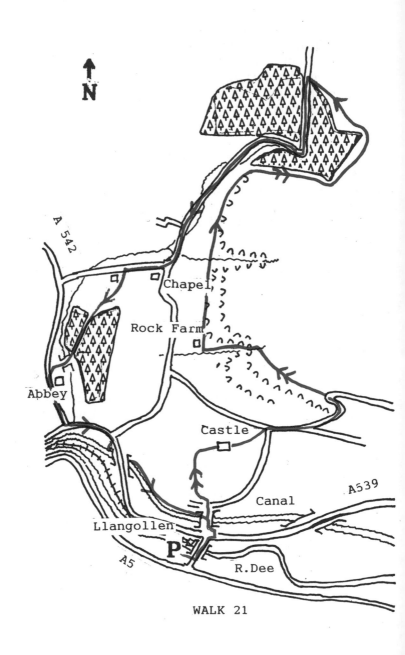

N

A 542

Chapel

Rock Farm

Abbey

Castle

A539

Canal

Llangollen

P

A5

R.Dee

WALK 21

lane but go slightly left, a little uphill. After 100m/ 110yd track through heather becomes clear again. Follow to lane and turn left.

100m/110yd turn left up wide track which leads direct to TP on Moel Morfydd. Massive erosion from this point caused by illegal, off-road driving and motorcycling. Follow track all the way over successive summits until carpark can be seen. Directions are: NE to Moel y Gaer; E to col and Moel y Gamelin; NNE to col beyond Cribin Oernant. From here the original walkers' path can be seen going NE over the S flank of Moel y Fan and is to be preferred to the eroded track. From this last summit go E and then N, down to carpark.

It is not practicable to shorten this walk.

21. World's End

Ordnance Survey Map No: 117
Distance from city centre: 82km/51ml
Walking distance: 20km/12.5ml
Amount of climbing: 470m/1550ft

An interesting walk which combines an opportunity to view antiquities with dramatic limestone scenery and screes in attractive countryside.

Park in centre of Llangollen off Market St. SJ214420. To get there use the Wallasey tunnel, M53 towards Chester and A55 and A483 to Wrexham and Ruabon. At Ruabon turn right on to the A539 to Llangollen. In town centre turn left over river bridge. Market St is a short distance on right.

Walk from carpark back to bridge and cross river and then main road. Turn right and then immediately left up a lane, over canal and up steps. Follow footpath signposted Castell Dinas Bran. After steep climb to castle continue NE through ruins and steeply down again to stile in field corner.

Turn right on lane, ignoring fork to right. Lane bends sharply left and back to right. Just on right bend turn NW on rough track on left. Where track curves right

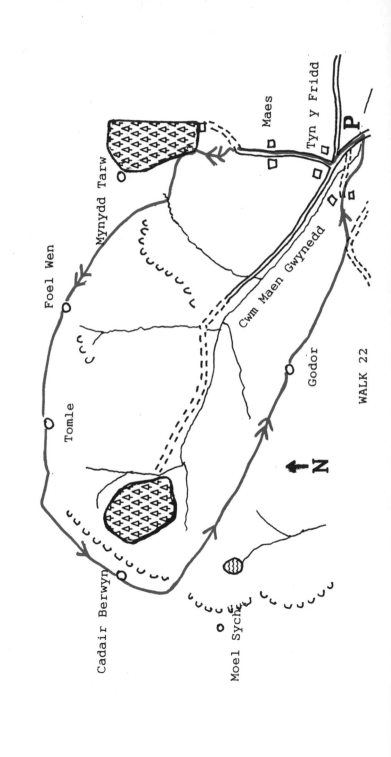

keep ahead NW on the edge of the crags until, 3km/ 1.9ml from lane, a cross track leads left down a ravine to Rock Farm. Turn right and continue on an exhilarating, high-level traverse to a wood. Go uphill and follow the wood down and round to a lane. The top of the wood is World's End.

Turn left downhill on lane and take second lane on right with a chapel on corner. After 1km/0.6ml take footpath left by a house and follow it through a wood, down to river, over a footbridge, through a caravan site and on to the A542. Turn left past the ruins of Valle Crucis Abbey and stay on road until canal bridge gives access to towpath. Follow towpath on left back to town.

To shorten this walk turn left at Rock Farm and follow lanes back to Llangollen. Save 10km/6.25ml.

22. *The Berwyns*

Ordnance Survey Map No: 125
Distance from city centre: 99km/62ml
Walking distance: 16km/10ml
Amount of climbing: 727m/2400ft

It is well worth the tortuous drive to this remote area for a walk which reveals the rocky crags of the eastern side of the Berwyns.

Park off the roadside near the farm of Tyn y Ffridd, 6.5km/4ml SW of Llanarmon Dyffryn Ceiriog in the valley of Cwm Maen Gwynedd. SJ118308. To get there take the Wallasey tunnel, M53 to J12 and A55 and A483 to Oswestry, Wrexham and Ruabon. Turn right on to the A5 4.8km/3ml S of Ruabon and after 1.6km/ 1ml turn left on to the B4500 to Llanarmon D.C. Continue over crossroads in village, over the hill and down to the telephone box at road junction. Parking spaces limited.

Take lane N from telephone box, through farmyard of Maes and keep straight on where lane bends right, heading for wood to gain summit of Mynydd Tarw. Follow a fence NW over Foel Wen and Tomle to a

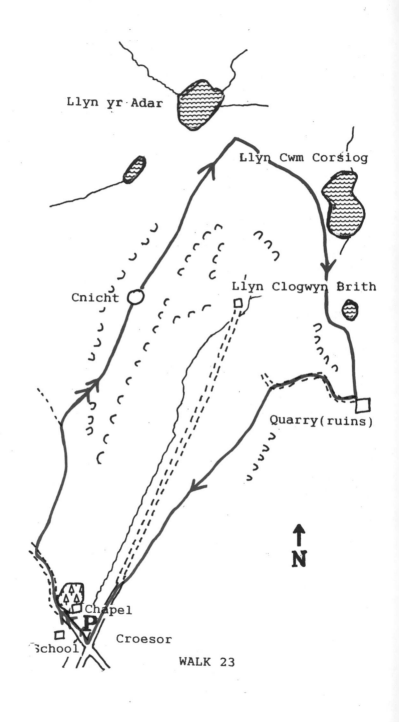

Llyn yr Adar

Llyn Cwm Corsiog

Llyn Clogwyn Brith

Cnicht

Quarry(ruins)

N

Chapel

P

School

Croesor

WALK 23

gate at a col where a prehistoric track crosses. Turn SSE, still following a fence to the triangulation station on Cadair Berwyn, previously thought to be the highest point. The fence leads 300m/0.2ml to the next peak, now recognised as such, and then over a col to Moel Sych, an excellent viewpoint.

Return to the col and turn SE towards Moel yr Ewig and Godor going down a gully and meeting a fence again. Follow this except where it curves right. From the summit of Godor go E down the ridge to the footpath which leads NE to car parking.

This walk may be shortened by going S on the ancient trackway beyond Tomle. Save 4.4km/2.25ml.

23. Cnicht

Ordnance Survey Maps Nos: 115/124 or OL Nos 17/18
Distance from city centre: 155km/97ml
Walking distance: 10.5km/6.5ml
Amount of climbing: 579m/1911ft
A small but imposing peak known from its shape as the Matterhorn of Wales. A good high-level walk follows.

Park in Croesor village. SH631447. To get there take the Wallasey tunnel, M53 to J5, A550/A494 to Ewloe, A55 to Llandudno Junction, A470 to Betws y Coed, A4086 to Pen y Gwryd and A498 to Beddgelert. There turn left over bridge (to Portmadoc) and 1.6km/1ml S of Beddgelert turn left over bridge on to A4085 (Barmouth). After a further 4.8km/3ml take the third minor lane on left to Croesor.

Turn right out of the carpark up the lane past the school and on to a track. Take a right fork (white waymarker) and make for the ridge of Cnicht ahead. After 0.8km/0.4ml leave main track which turns left and cross a ladder stile to right to gain the ridge which leads to the summit.

Continue NE along ridge towards Llyn yr Adar. A large cairn marks the turning point SE. The track, indistinct at times, is cairned to Llyn cwm Corsiog and

73

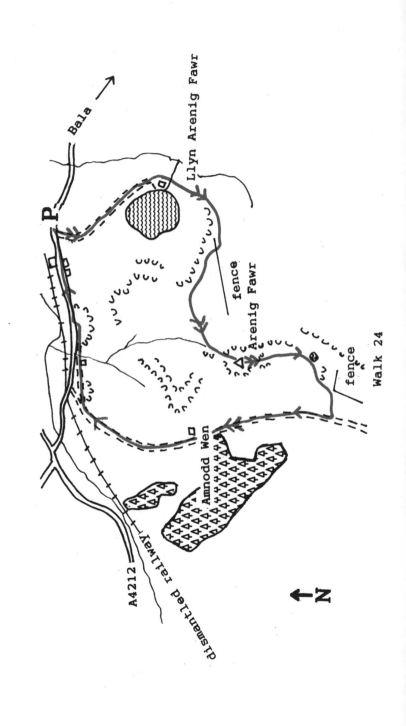

SNOWDONIA AND NORTH WALES

Llyn Clogwyn Brith and then down to the disused slate quarry.

Turn right by the quarry buildings to follow a disused railway track, leaving it just before it curves right for a track on left. This is indistinct at first but improves and is easily followed downhill to a lane. Turn left and then right at the T-junction for the carpark.

It is not practicable to shorten this walk except by retracing your steps from the summit of Cnicht. Save 4.5km/2.8ml.

24. *Arenig Fawr*

Ordnance Survey Map No: 124 or OL No 18
Distance from city centre: 99km/62ml
Walking distance: 12.8km/8ml
Amount of climbing: 583m/1924ft

· For me Arenig Fawr is a gem. It has a superbly rocky summit which cannot be seen until near at hand and in clear autumn weather provides the ultimate viewpoint for the hills of North and Mid-Wales. It is, however, in a very rainy area and it is worth being sure of the weather before setting out. Navigation is difficult in poor conditions.

Park on the wide verge of minor road 10km/6ml W of Bala. SH845395. To get there take the Wallasey tunnel, M53 to J5 and A550/A594 to junction with A55. Take A55 (Wrexham) turning at next exit on to A550 (Wrexham) and then A5104 (Corwen). Turn left on to A494, right on to A5 and left on to A494 again. After crossing river on outskirts of Bala take first right – A4212 – and just past 30 mph sign turn left on to minor road to Llidiardau. Park on right 1km/0.6ml past second cattle grid after Llidiardau, near gate and stile on left giving access to rough, stony track.

Cross stile and follow track to S end of lake. Follow white waymark leading to gate at back of stone hut. Cross stream by iron ladder bridge (on all fours if stream swollen) and follow small but well-trodden path up ridge, through gap in wire fence and over rise where

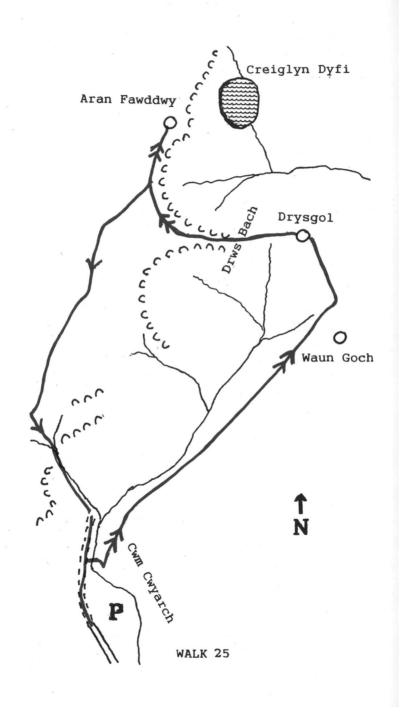

Creiglyn Dyfi

Aran Fawddwy

Drysgol

Drws Bach

Waun Goch

N

Cwm Cwyarch

P

WALK 25

summit comes into view. After a few m/yd cross fence on right using handily placed rocks and follow path contouring hillside. This passes beneath a crag and just past a spring a few cairns lead up to summit ridge. Track is intermittent so pick easiest way through rocks. On ridge turn left and follow line of broken fence to TP and memorial to US aircrew.

Follow line of fence S over minor peak and down scree slope. Just past little tarn in col turn right at base of small crag to pick up path going SW. When this meets corner of fence coming downhill on left, turn right past ruins of stone sheepfold below – no path – and go down very steep grassy slope to track. Turn right.

Past ruined farm, track becomes grassy and rises slightly. Stony section that follows often has stream in but is dry again beyond the gate. Fork right at small, disused quarry on green track contouring hillside. Past red brick ruins cross stile into disused quarry and go through gate on to road. Turn right for car parking.

To shorten this walk go NW from summit and then N into hollow by Craig yr Hyrddod on map to pass between crags and reach W side of quarry. This saves 3.2km/2ml, but is not advised in mist.

25. *Aran Fawddwy*

Ordnance Survey Map No: 125 or OL No 23
Distance from city centre: 155km/97ml
Walking distance: 12km/7.5ml
Amount of climbing: 768m/2534ft

Access to this superb mountain range is disputed so it is important to keep to the rights of way and the permissive paths that have been agreed.

Park on the roadside at the end of a minor lane N of Dinas Mawddwy. SH854185. To get there take the Wallasey tunnel, M53 to J12 and A55/A483 to Wrexham and Oswestry. S of Oswestry turn right on to A495, right at its junction with A458 and right again at Mallwyd on to A470. After 2.4km/1.5ml turn right

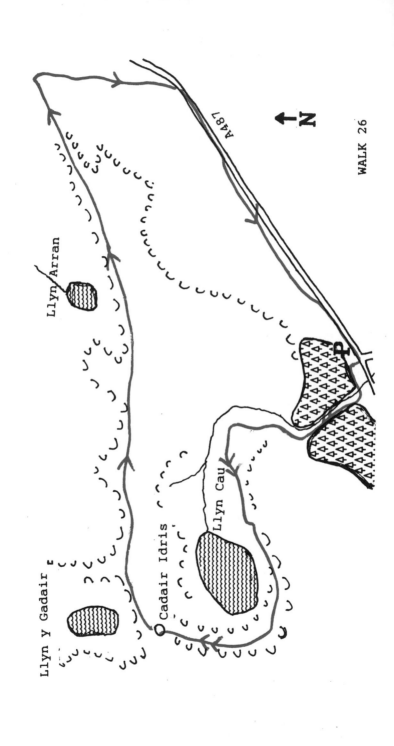

Llyn y Gadair

Cadair Idris

Llyn Cau

Llyn y Arran

A487

N

WALK 26

P

in Dinas Mawddwy and take the lane on left just across river. Parking in 4.8km/3ml.

The walk starts a short way up the road where a bridge on right, signposted to the Arans, leads to a lane and then a track which climbs the open hillside NE to the col between Waun Goch and Drysgol. At a white post here go N with a wire fence on the right along ridge which narrows and leads to a large cairn. Follow the fence NW, cross a stile and bear right to the summit.

Retrace your steps to the ladder stile and continue SW to a cross track in the col, following a fence all the way. Turn left at the col and follow the waymarked track down a sometimes steep and rocky path SE to the lane and car parking.

Because of restrictions on access it is not possible to vary this route.

26. *Cadair Idris*

Ordnance Survey Map No: 124 or OL No 23
Distance from city centre: 125km/78ml
Walking distance: 17km/10.5ml
Amount of climbing: 1030m/3400ft

Of all the ways up Cadair Idris this is considered by many to be the best. As the mountain is near the sea it is notorious for bad weather and this walk is best reserved for a fine day.

Carpark just off A487 at Minffordd. SH732116. To get there take the Wallasey tunnel, M53 to J5, A550 to Queensferry and A494 to Mold, Ruthin, Bala and Dolgellau. Turn left on to A470 3.2km/2ml before Dolgellau and follow to Machynlleth and then turn right at Cross Foxes on to the A487. At the bottom of the hill, Minffordd, the B4405 forks right. At the junction is a lane on right leading to carpark.

Go through gate at W end of carpark, follow the track left and then right to the entrance to the nature reserve. Climb steeply through the woods and follow the cairns with the stream from Llyn Cau to right. The path curves round crags before the ridge can be gained by going S. Once on ridge keep to cliff-tops direct to summit. N of triangulation station is a substantial shelter.

Continue NNE over Mynnydd Moel and Gau Graig, always keeping to the highest ground. After 2.5km/ 1.6ml a wall is met. This is almost continuous for another 2.5km/1.6ml and leads down to a track on the far side of a small wood. Here turn right and descend to the A487. Turn right and after 1km/0.6ml join a bridleway on right which leads back to the road not far from the carpark.

This walk can be shortened only by retracing your steps from the summit. Save 7km/4.5ml.

Walk 19   Brenig Reservoir

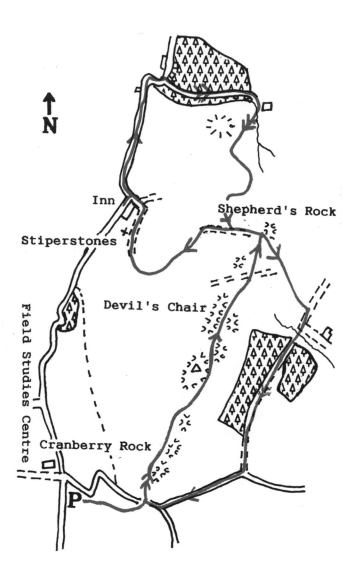

N

Inn

Shepherd's Rock

Stiperstones

Devil's Chair

Field Studies Centre

Cranberry Rock

P

Walk 27

SHROPSHIRE AND THE MARCHES

27. The Stiperstones

Ordnance Survey Map Nos: 126 and 137
Distance from city centre: 138km/86ml
Walking distance: 12km/7.5ml
Amount of climbing: 450m/1485ft
The Stiperstones is an interesting and beautiful area. After 100 years, the many old lead mines are now revegetated and the valleys are as great an attraction as the impressive quartz tors on the hilltop. The district was used by Mary Webb as the setting for her novel *The Golden Arrow*, and there are many legends associated with the rocks.

Use the public car park at The Bog near Stiperstones village. SO355977. To get there take the Wallasey tunnel, M53, bypassing Chester and A55/A483, bypassing Wrexham, Ruabon and Oswestry. On bypass turn on to A5 to new Shrewsbury bypass and take A488 (Bishops Castle). After 11.5km/7ml beyond Pontesbury take minor road on left by telephone box, signposted Shelve and The Bog. Turn right at T-junction and fork left past Field Studies Centre. Large carpark on right.

At top edge of carpark signpost points uphill past pond and through scrub to stile. Cross and follow power lines to next stile. Go half left to road, cross to stile and climb to top of hill with impressive rock outcrops. Go over crossing track and continue to large cairn just before last outcrop (Shepherd's Rock on right). Turn left and follow track down past spoil heaps and cottages to road. Inn and shop just to left.

Turn right to follow road for 1km/0.6ml. Road turns sharply right and then left. On left bend take lane on right by corrugated-iron garage. Lane becomes track, passing old cottages in wood, and finally turning right, crossing stream and passing last cottage on left. Shortly, stream is crossed again and you are now on path in narrowing valley. At top, ground drops away steeply and cross track is met. Turn left. Follow path around head of valley, turning half-left over spoil heap at far side before continuing S on faint path to join outward track to village. Turn left to cairn by Shepherd's Rock.

Walk 28   The Long Mynd from the west

Walk 27   The Stiperstones

Take track SE, dropping to gate at edge of National Nature Reserve. Continue on track to second gate and then go half-right down to farm track. When this bends left keep going SW to cross stream and enter wood. Track comes out at carpark and road. Turn right and right at T-junction. After 25m/20yd cross stile on left and retrace outward route to carpark.

This walk may be shortened by turning left at inn and walking to end of village, where stile by private garage on left leads to path through wood to left and on to lower slopes of hill. On open moorland turn right and follow derelict stone wall on right until reaching road. Save 2.4km/1.5ml.

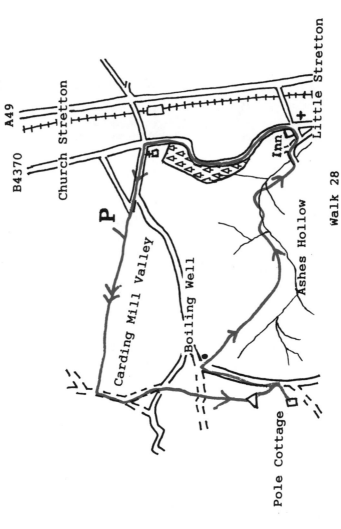

A49

B4370

Church Stretton

P

Carding Mill Valley

Boiling Well

Pole Cottage

Ashes Hollow

Inn

Little Stretton

Walk 28

28. *The Long Mynd*

Ordnance Survey Map No: 137
Distance from city centre: 138km/86ml
Walking distance: 13km/8ml
Amount of climbing: 220m/725ft

As on the Stiperstones, one of the best features of the Long Mynd is the great number of deep valleys and this walk includes the most popular as well as one of the loveliest of these, joined by a stretch of high ground. The return is by a quiet lane.

Park in the National Trust carpark in Carding Mill Valley (members free). SO441948. To get there take the Wallasey tunnel, M53, bypassing Chester, and A55/A483, bypassing Wrexham, Ruabon and Oswestry. On bypass turn on to A5 to new Shrewsbury bypass and take A49 to Church Stretton. Turn right at traffic lights into town and right on to B4370. Carpark is signposted up road to left.

From carpark go NW uphill, keeping to main valley until track on top is reached. Do not take side valleys. Turn left.

After 400m/0.25ml take track on left to metalled road. Cross to path almost directly opposite and continue across stony track and past TP down to road again. Turn right to grassy patch with trees and iron barn (Pole Cottage) – a good place for lunch.

From cottage turn left on road going NE for 1.1km/0.7ml to bend in road where track joins from left and Boiling Well, green marshy area, is on right. Turn S into valley and follow track through Ashes Hollow, crossing stream several times.

Track emerges on B4370 near inn. Turn left for Church Stretton. Past church go up lane on left and over crossroads. Take track which forks right after last houses. This contours to road in Carding Mill Valley. Turn left for carpark.

This walk can be shortened by continuing downhill on road past Boiling Well. Watch for track going back sharp left before houses are reached. Save 4km/2.5ml.

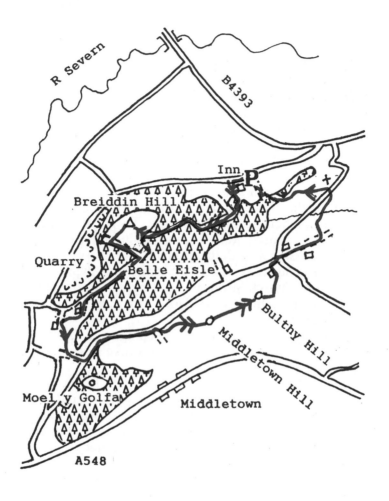

R Severn

B4393

Inn **P**

Breiddin Hill

Quarry

Belle Eisle

Bulthy Hill

Middletown Hill

Moel y Golfa

Middletown

A548

N

Walk 29

29. The Breidden Hills

Ordnance Survey Map No: 126
Distance from city centre: 120km/75ml
Walking distance: 12km/7.5ml
Amount of climbing: 590m/1950ft

For most walkers, their first and only sight of the Breidden Hills, surmounted by Rodney's Pillar, is as they walk Offa's Dyke. The hills, which are volcanic in origin and rise in a spectacular fashion from the Severn plain, can be seen from the Peckforton Hills (Walk 1). The landlady at the Admiral Rodney assures me that in clear weather you can see Liverpool docks from the summit, so if you haven't seen Liverpool docks, you know where to come.

Park with permission at the Admiral Rodney near Welshpool. SJ311411. To get there take the Wallasey tunnel and M53, A55 and A483 (Oswestry and Welshpool) to Four Crosses. Turn left on to B4393 (Shrewsbury) and after 6.5km/4ml turn right on to minor road signposted Criggion and Rodney's Pillar. Carpark on left after 1 km/0.5ml.

From carpark turn left and go through first gate on left. Go uphill on right-hand edge of field, cross one stile and then another ahead which leads into wood. Track, faint at first, improves and leads to forestry track. Turn left and near end of plantation turn right on bridleway. (Extensive signposting is being undertaken and route described may be waymarked by publication date.)

After 200m/220yd turn left on waymarked path, cross stile at end of plantation and follow waymarks up to summit. Turn left to walk W on ridge, skirting edge of quarry on right to reach stony track going downhill. Turn right in front of plantation and continue down to forestry track and gate on left. Turn right. Track leads through gate into forest for 2km/1.25ml, emerging by gate. Turn left, crossing cattle-grid on to farm track. Pass farm on right and follow waymarked route over stiles down to next farm track. Turn left and cross stile in corner on left opposite farm. Continue with hedge/ fence on right, cross stream and make for marker post in middle of field. Turn slightly left to find stile into small wood. At this point waymarking ends. Go half-right down to stream bed and at gap in wire go up zigzags on right-hand bank and then ahead to cross iron fence on to grassy lane. Turn left to reach lane and turn left again.

Where hedges end, turn right on waymarked path contouring at first and then going up to summit of Middletown Hill. Continue NE to descend, go through gate and climb Bulthy Hill. From summit go E through bracken to join footpath below. Turn left and with hedge/wire fence on right continue through gate to pass Bulthy cottage on left and reach lane. In quick succession turn right, then left at junction and then right on lane by Yew Tree Farm on left.

Lane passes below Kempster's Hill on left and reaches gate where metalling ends. Go through gate and down through trees to stream and gate. Go half-right by right-hand edge of field to lane. Cross and go over stile with small chapel (Bethel 1875) to right. Route now WSW with wood on right at first leading to forestry track through natural woodland. When denser woods reached by old wire fence, turn sharp right down edge of open meadow and then pass beneath trees to stile. Cross, turn left for a few m/yd until derelict corrugated-iron buildings can be seen to right. Turn right to pass between these and then right on track beyond leading to lane. Carpark can be seen on left.

To shorten this walk do not go through gate to ascend Bulthy Hill. Turn left down to lane, cross and pass through Belle Eisle Farm opposite. At end of enclosed track, bridleway follows hedge to right to gate. Go through and then left to ford. Cross, go through gate and follow path with plantation to right to forestry track. Turn right and retrace outward route, remembering to enter wood on sharp left turn. Save 2km/1.25ml.

Walk 16   The burial chamber

Walk 17   Conwy Mountain

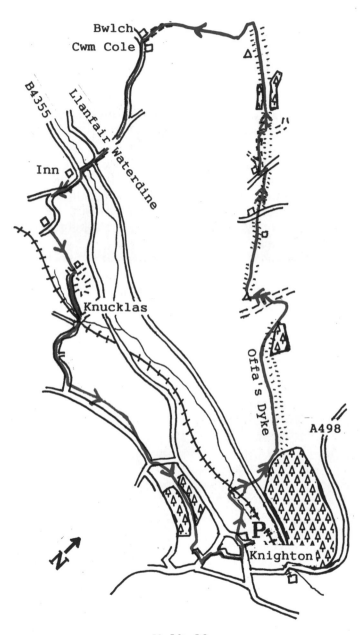

Walk 30

30. *Offa's Dyke from Knighton*

Ordnance Survey Map No: 137
Distance from city centre: 152km/95ml
Walking distance: 22.5km/14ml
Amount of climbing: 660m/2200ft

A superb day out over not only the highest but also the best-preserved section of the Dyke, returning by footpaths, woods and quiet lanes.

Park in Knighton near the Youth Hostel and Information Centre. SO285725. To get there take the Wallasey tunnel, M53, A55, A483 to Welshpool and A490 to Knighton. Pass railway station, turn right at T-junction and pass clock-tower on left. Parking is signposted on right.

Return to road from carpark, turn right to pass hostel and right again into park. Offa's Dyke is well waymarked with yellow arrows and/or white acorns. Go half-left across field, turn left on riverbank and at end of hedge on right go up to lane. Cross and go uphill. At top turn left on narrow but clear path which follows Offa's Dyke NW for 6.5km/4ml, mostly with fence on right on top and with numerous stiles.

After first TP drop steeply to farm and lane; turn left and then right over stile. Cross two bridges to next lane and go through farm gate opposite and on left. Take right-hand fork and after second gate walk on top of dyke until sign directs you to walk on green lane left to preserve dyke. Go through gate across lane at this point and then through gate next to it on W side to leave dyke altogether. Go SW to reach another gate and then go downhill, keeping to crest of ridge. After two more gates enclosed track leads down to burnt-out ruins of Bwlch Farm on lane. Turn left, passing restored Cwm Cole, perhaps picking up a brochure from Mrs Lewis, and follow lane down.

At junction turn left and then right to cross bridge to B4355. Turn left and take first lane on right. At fork go left. At brow of hill turn left on track between hedges. Keep ahead through gate at fork and walk

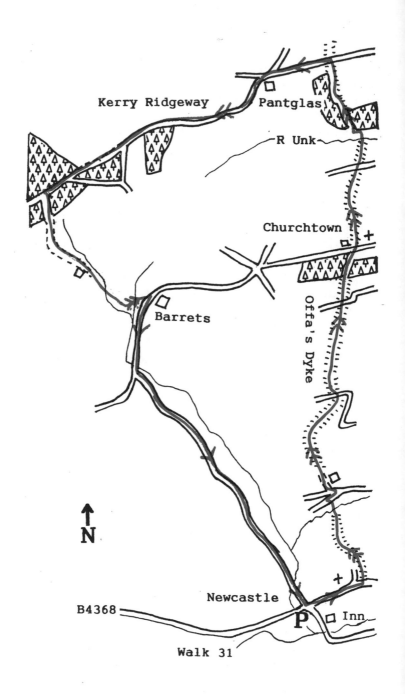

Kerry Ridgeway

Pantglas

R Unk

Churchtown

Offa's Dyke

Barrets

N

Newcastle

B4368

P

Inn

Walk 31

with hedge on right across field, past sheepfold and corrugated-iron shed to track. Turn right and continue downhill when track is metalled. At T-junction turn right, cross stream and go beneath railway viaduct to right. Turn immediately left up small lane. Pass junction on left and at T-junction at top of steep hill turn left on green track with hedge/fence on left for 1.2km/0.75ml on to lane. Turn left and left again at T-junction. In 20m/25yd fork right at footpath sign in Welsh (Llwybr Cyhoeddus) on to track leading into wood and contouring hillside. Ignore small tracks off. Path leads into open field above new housing estate and continues half-left to officially diverted route with stile in field corner. Cross stile and turn left to new path down. Go left on first road and right by telephone box to reach main road.

Turn right into Market Street and left down High Street to clock-tower. Turn left for carpark.

This walk may be shortened by turning left along lane leading to Knighton, instead of crossing bridge to B4355. Save 1km/0.75ml and 220m/730ft of climbing.

31. The Kerry Ridgeway

Ordnance Survey Map No: 137
Distance from city centre: 147km/92ml
Walking distance: 21km/13ml
Amount of climbing: 425m/1400ft

A walk in three sections: a strenuous section of Offa's Dyke path with many ups and downs, a walk along one of Britain's oldest tracks, the Kerry Ridgeway, and a return by a quiet country lane.

Park in Newcastle village. SO246823. To get there take the Wallasey tunnel, M53, A55, A483 to Welshpool and A490 to Clun. Turn right on B4368 to Newcastle. Cross bridge and pass inn on right. Adequate parking on W side of crossroads – take care not to block gates. More parking on verge by church.

From crossroads go E along Church Lane, passing church on left and turn left to cross stile at Offa's Dyke sign just past road junction on left. Offa's Dyke is well marked (see Walk 30). After farm gate, best route up hill is under trees on top of dyke. At bottom of hill cross stream and go half-left to stile on lane, turn right then left at junction and right to pass farm. After farm, wood is entered by stile; after leaving wood track forks – go right to stile above. Follow waymarking through Churchtown and down to R. Unk. Turn left on far bank of river to find stile on right and go up steeply through wood to lane which forms metalled section of Kerry Ridgeway. Turn left.

After 1km/0.75ml fork left by Pant Glas Farm. On reaching sign, "Unsuitable for Motors", keep straight ahead. Track improves for walkers and continues toward plantation on skyline. On reaching lane, fork right on Ridgeway with plantation on left.

Ridgeway enters plantation and becomes forest track. At fork go left and just after track joins from right take track on left to gate at edge of plantation. Pass through gate and follow stony track down to building, beyond which it becomes grassy and then peters out. Follow direction of power lines down to gate and track beyond through bracken. Track goes through several gates and over crossing tracks, finally going uphill to grey buildings on skyline. Turn right on lane. At bottom of hill take turning on left signposted to Newcastle and follow it directly to crossroads.

To shorten this walk, go W at Churchtown, turn left at crossroads, take first turning on right and go right at T-junction. At bottom of hill turn right to pass church and reach car parking. Save 6km/3.75ml.

Walk 15   Drum and Foel Fras

Walk 38   En route to Lose Hill

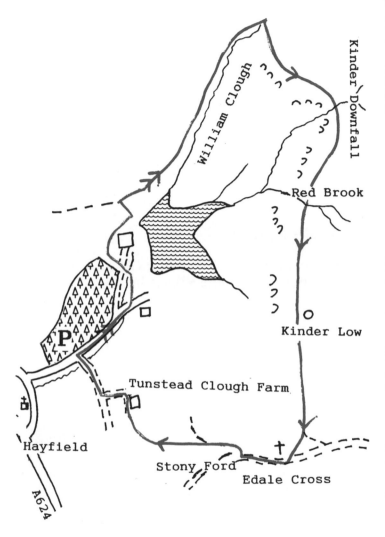

Kinder Downfall

William Clough

Red Brook

Kinder Low

P

Tunstead Clough Farm

Hayfield

A624

Stony Ford

Edale Cross

N

Walk 32

THE PEAK DISTRICT

32. Kinder Downfall

Ordnance Survey Map No: 110 or OL No 1
Distance from city centre: 85km/53ml
Walking distance: 13.5km/8.5ml
Amount of climbing: 460m/1518ft
    This walk includes a strenuous climb to the waterfall of Kinder Downfall and then traverses the rim of the plateau, following part of the Pennine Way and part of its alternative start. Conditions can be bad and good weather is needed to enjoy the walk fully.
    Park by Bowden Bridge on road from Hayfield to Kinder Reservoir. Further parking towards Hayfield. SK048869. To get there take M62/M63 to Stockport (J12), A6 (Whaley Bridge) and A6015 through New Mills to Hayfield. Cross A624 into village and turn left. Past church take Kinder Road E. Parking is in 1.5km/0.8ml on left.
    From carpark continue up access road, turning right to cross stream and go past farm. Turn left at junction, down towards reservoir buildings and turn right again to pass above them. Path goes up left to join another track. Turn right to contour above reservoir. Gradually path enters William Clough with a choice of ways within it, all leading to two cairns and then Pennine Way (PW) signpost on edge of Kinder Plateau.
    Turn right and walk along edge to Kinder Downfall,

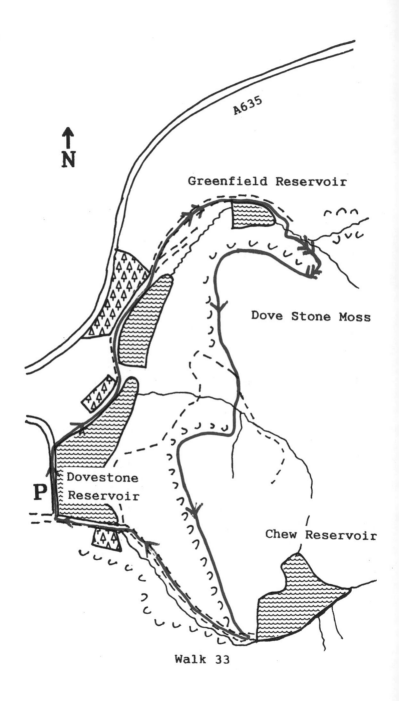

N

A635

Greenfield Reservoir

Dove Stone Moss

Dovestone
Reservoir

P

Chew Reservoir

Walk 33

continuing SSW beyond it on PW alternative. Route is cairned, crossing Red Brook to large cairn by TP on Kinder Low. Path turns slightly left away from edge going now SSE until it reaches a wall. Follow wall round hillside to sheepfold. Cross stile and then go through gateway on to large track. On right is medi-aeval Edale Cross.

Follow track W, cross stream (Oaken Clough) at Stony Ford and in a few metres go over stile on right to pick up path to Hayfield. At next fork go left and follow path to Tunstead Clough Farm over series of stiles. Route is waymarked to left of farmhouse on to access road. Follow this down to right to carpark.

It is not practicable to shorten this walk.

33. Dove Stone Moss

Ordnance Survey Map No: 110 or OL No 1
Distance from city centre: 74km/46ml
Walking distance: 14km/8.5ml
Amount of climbing: 257m/850ft

This walk is right in the NW corner of the Peak District National Park. It skirts some very attractive reservoirs and rises to an escarpment lined with crags, along which it contours before dropping down a deep valley to the starting point.

Park on the W bank of Dove Stone Reservoir. SE013034. To get there take the M62/M602 to Manchester and A635 through Ashton-under-Lyne and Stalybridge towards Holmfirth. Turn right down minor road to reservoir and sailing club 2km/1ml past junction with A669 on left. Carpark is on right.

From carpark go N along road parallel to reservoir, continuing on NW bank up to next reservoir – Yeoman Hey. Stay on W bank taking left fork which leads to Greenfield Reservoir. Follow the N bank going E and cross to S side of stream on reaching bridge. Take right-hand stream when valley forks. Note the crags above on right and when crags peter out and gradient on right lessens, go up right to top of hill.

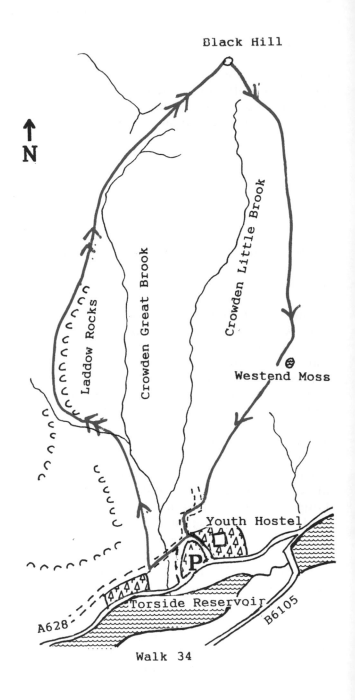

Black Hill

N

Laddow Rocks

Crowden Great Brook

Crowden Little Brook

Westend Moss

Youth Hostel

P

Torside Reservoir

A628

B6105

Walk 34

Follow path W along top of crags. Path turns S away from edge for some distance and is joined by track coming in from right. When it turns SE to follow stream, turn NW to follow edge of escarpment again. This turns S for 5km/2.75ml and then E to Chew Reservoir. Go to S end of dam where access road leads W down the valley. Take left fork near bottom to reach Dove Stone Reservoir again.

This walk can be shortened by taking the path that comes in from right. Save 5km/3ml.

34. Laddow Rocks and Black Hill

Ordnance Survey Map No: 110 or OL No 1
Distance from city centre: 88km/55ml
Walking distance: 13.75km/8.5ml
Amount of climbing: 615m/2030ft

This walk follows the route of the present day Pennine Way to Black Hill and returns by what was the original Pennine Way, in Wainwright's view a superior route. You will be able to judge for yourself. It is worth heeding his opinion in the *Pennine Way Companion* that the summit is a dangerous place in bad weather and that it should not be attempted alone. In an emergency the nearest route off is E to the Holme Moss TV transmitter on the A6024. The going on top is tough.

Park near Crowden Youth Hostel. SK072993. To get there take M62/M63/M66/M67 to Mottram-in-Longendale. Then take A57/A628 (Barnsley and Sheffield) and parking is on left near E end of Torside Reservoir, before B6105 joins from right.

From carpark take lane which goes NW then SW to join Pennine Way near top of small wood. Turn right and follow Pennine Way N over top of Laddow Rocks. Path drops and follows Crowden Brook N then NE for a further 1.6km/1ml over marshy ground to summit.

From summit walk on bearing of 150° for 1.4km/0.9ml before turning S along narrowing ridge to plateau of White Low a further 1km/0.6ml away. Here follow

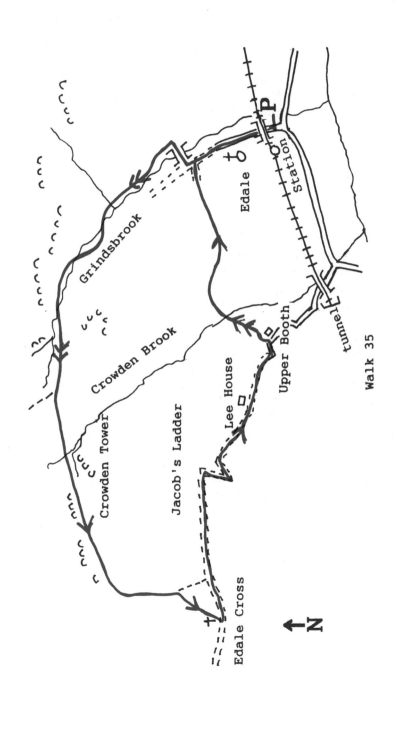

Grindsbrook

Crowden Brook

Crowden Tower

Jacob's Ladder

Lee House

Upper Booth

Edale

station

tunnel

P

Edale Cross

Walk 35

N

path SW past small tarn on Westend Moss before dropping down to right of ridge into Crowden.

This walk may be shortened by turning S at the N
end of Laddow Rocks and returning at foot of crags to
carpark. Save 4.5km/2.8ml.

35. *Grindsbrook and Jacob's Ladder*

Ordnance Survey Map No: 110 or OL No 1
Distance from city centre: 95km/59ml
Walking distance: 12km/7.5ml
Amount of climbing: 545m/1798ft

Walk the first few miles of the Pennine Way (PW)
and return by the packhorse track that forms the alternative start. The route passes a number of curiously
weathered outcrops on the edge of the plateau. Not to
be attempted in poor visibility.

Park near railway station S of Edale. SK124853.
To get there take M62/M602 to Stockport J12, A6 to
Chapel-en-le-Frith and A625 towards Hope. After
6km/3.75ml turn left by wood on minor road to Edale.
Turn left into village. Carpark is on right before
station.

From carpark go N into village, under railway and
past church on left. Continue on track and turn right
at PW sign to cross stream among trees. Follow well-
waymarked track 4km/2.5ml NW up Grindsbrook to
reach plateau. When PW turns N, cross stream and
turn left up to Crowden Tower, the first of the outcrops
on the route.

Path goes around rim of plateau W and then SW,
passing other outcrops before meeting PW alternative
by wall. Follow wall S to packhorse track by Edale
Cross, which is just to the right. Turn left on the track
and follow it down the steep steps of Jacob's Ladder,
over stream and on to Lee Farm and then Upper
Booth. Turn left through farm and go through gate on
right to follow signposted path uphill at first to Edale.
At lane turn right to reach carpark.

It is not practicable to shorten this walk.

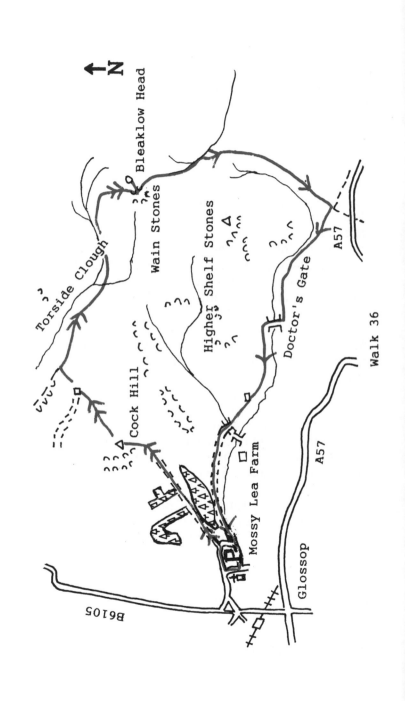

N

Bleaklow Head

Torside Clough

Wain Stones

Higher Shelf Stones

Cock Hill

Doctor's Gate

A57

Mossy Lea Farm

B6105

Glossop

A57

Walk 36

36. Bleaklow Head

Ordnance Survey Map No: 110 or OL No 1
Distance from city centre: 88km/55ml
Walking distance: 16km/10ml
Amount of climbing: 503m/1660ft

This walk takes in what used to be one of the less appealing sections of the Pennine Way. A stone causeway laid in 1992 enables the walker to admire the vast landscape instead of ploughing through the morass, although there is still enough left to satisfy the masochist. The route uses an old quarry track at the start and a Roman road to finish. Not a route for misty conditions.

Park opposite the Wheatsheaf near Old Glossop church. SK042949. To get there take M62/M6/M56 (Stockport) and M66, M67, A57 (Sheffield) to Glossop. At traffic lights in town centre turn left on B6105 past railway station on left. After 1.5km/0.9ml turn right at crossroads and right at T-junction. Where road bends right to church go straight ahead. Parking on right. Other parking near bus turning-circle at end of walk.

Turn right from carpark, left at junction and fork left up Charles St to stile. Cross and follow enclosed track for 4km/2.5ml. Cross wire fence ahead and follow track going half-right beyond to TP on Cock Hill. Faint path NE leads along ridge to little summit with ruined shooting lodge (butts on right). Continue NE for 300m/350yd to meet Pennine Way on edge of ravine. Turn right and follow Pennine Way (no waymarking) E and then S to Wainstones on Bleaklow Head summit. (Route often deep inside eroded grough.)

To pick up route S look for two stone posts in line leading into deep grough. Route is marked now by stone posts and some paving. After 4km/2.5ml, within 400m/0.25ml of A57, rough track crosses just before wooden marker. Turn right and follow this track down into valley.

Pass through first gate near farm left and cross bridge on right. Farm track leads to bus turning-circle. Follow

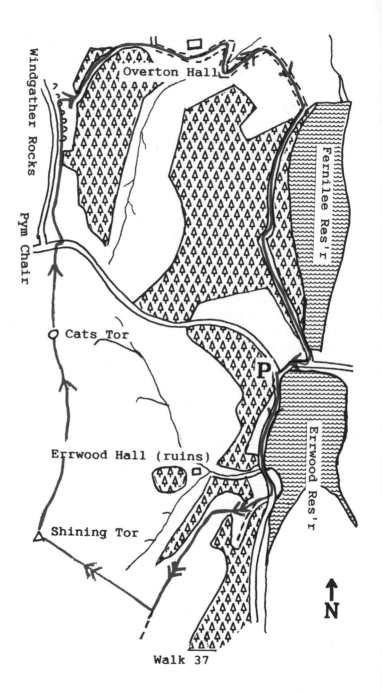

Windgather Rocks

Pym Chair

Overton Hall

Fernilee Res'r

Cats Tor

P

Errwood Hall (ruins)

Errwood Res'r

Shining Tor

N

Walk 37

road past factory right to T-junction. Turn right and pass church to reach carpark.

It is not practicable to shorten this walk.

37. *Shining Tor*

Ordnance Survey Map No: 118 and 119 or OL No 24
Distance from city centre: 83km/52ml
Walking distance: 16km/10ml
Amount of climbing: 360m/1188ft

Water and woodland ensure the popularity of this area to the extent that the direct route in, by the road E of the Cat and Fiddle, has traffic restrictions. The route runs by Errwood Reservoir, over a ridge and past a rock-climbing area; it returns through a wood by the reservoirs.

Park near Errwood reservoir. SK013757. To get there take M62/M6 to J19, A5033 to Knutsford, A537 to Macclesfield and A537 (Buxton). After 8km/5ml turn left at crossroads, following signposts to Goyt Valley. Carpark at bottom of hill on right.

Go S along lane with reservoir on left, cross bridge and pass carpark on right. Cross road to signpost for Shining Tor at S end of carpark. This leads up ridge, crossing ladder stile and following wall on right to stone step stile on right where ground levels out. New gravel track leads to TP on Shining Tor. Turn right to follow wall on left over boggy ground for 3.5km/2ml to lane at Pym Chair. Cross and turn right to stile and path to wall by road. Turn right with wall on left, cross ladder stile and go over top of Windgather Rocks.

At far end of crag go over stile on right and follow waymarked route along edge of plantation. Turn right after next stile and follow fence on right turning corner to reach stile leading out of woods. Maintain direction with fence on right over rise. Path drops to end of lane. Cross and go along farm road opposite past Overton Hall. Road doubles back on itself, crosses stream and passes Knipe Farm on left before reaching reservoir. Turn right on road by dam and before bend cross stile

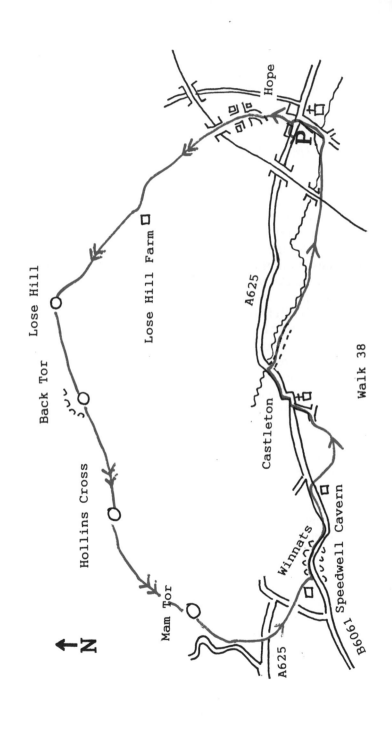

N

Lose Hill

Back Tor

Lose Hill Farm

Hollins Cross

Mam Tor

Castleton

Hope

P

A625

A625

Winnats

Speedwell Cavern

B6061

Walk 38

on left to path through plantation. Keep right at fork. Path crosses footbridge and descends to foot of dam. Climb right for road and carpark.

To shorten this walk turn right at Pym Chair to return direct to carpark. Save 4.5km/2.8ml.

38. Lose Hill and Mam Tor

Ordnance Survey Map No: 110 or OL No 1
Distance from city centre: 101km/63ml
Walking distance: 12km/7.5ml
Amount of climbing: 466m/1538ft

After a stiff climb, enjoy an exhilarating ridge walk before descending through a dramatic valley to Castleton and a quiet riverside walk to Hope.

Use the public carpark in Hope village on the S side of the A625. SK171835. To get there take the M62/M6 to J19, A537 to Macclesfield, B5470 to Chapel-en-le-Frith and A625 to Castleton and Hope.

From carpark cross road, turn right and take footpath on left between houses. This leads through housing and past school on right, always heading NW. Line of path is by a series of stiles, over railway line and across field to lane, before entering fields again. Lose Hill is in sight ahead and the route is well waymarked. By Losehill Farm a signpost half-right on skyline indicates route and the path from here is easily followed to summit.

From summit go SW along ridge for 3.5km/2ml with superb views in all directions as far as Mam Tor before descending by stone track towards road. Just before reaching it go left over stile, cross field, go over road and into next field and take left fork to road again. Cross and take path to left of farm.

At road (Winnats Pass) turn left and follow it until 25m/20yd past entrance to Speedwell Cavern and turn right along footpath which contours hillside to Castleton with wall on left. Descend to main road by church and turn right.

After last houses in Castleton a lane on right is

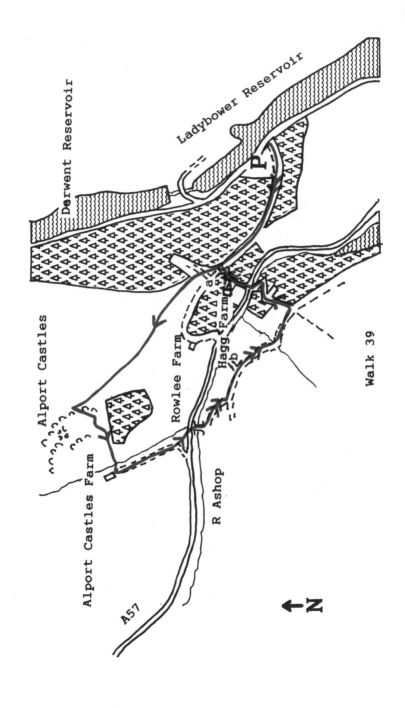

Derwent Reservoir

Ladybower Reservoir

P

Alport Castles

Alport Castles Farm

Rowlee Farm

Hagg Farm

a

b

R Ashop

A57

Walk 39

←N

signposted to Hope. It changes to a path, the line of which can be followed over stiles in an easterly direction. It crosses railway line and follows river to a lane. Turn left to Hope village and left at main road for carpark.

This walk can be shortened by taking a track S to Castleton from the ridge at Hollins Cross. Save 3km/ 1.9ml.

39. *Alport Castles*

Ordnance Survey Map No: 110 or OL No 1
Distance from city centre: 110km/69ml
Walking distance: 14.5km/9ml
Amount of climbing: 520m/1720ft

A gentle climb to a fine ridge leads to the interesting area of rocky landslip known as Alport Castles with views of Kinder Scout on left. The return is by the route of a Roman road.

Park in Bridge End carpark on W bank of Ladybower Reservoir. SK180885. To get there take M62/ M6/M56 (Stockport) and M66/M67/A57 (Sheffield) through Glossop. After 21km/13ml, just before viaduct, turn left at signpost for Derwent Valley. Carpark on left after 2.5km/1.5ml just beyond war memorial.

Go through gate at S end of carpark on to signposted packhorse route. Near top of hill track forks left to signpost at edge of plantation. Cross stile and follow edge of plantation on right in direction of Glossop. At end of plantation cross two stony tracks to reach ladder stile on skyline. Track leads through gate. Turn left on broad track with wall on left for short distance, keeping to edge of escarpment on left. After 3km/1.9ml, at end of short section of wall on left, go down track into hollow on left and over stile by signpost.

Follow track down and over stile on right. *Work on paths and fences in this area may lead to change of detail*. Track leads down to bridge. Cross and turn right to stile above on left. Follow waymarks and stiles to

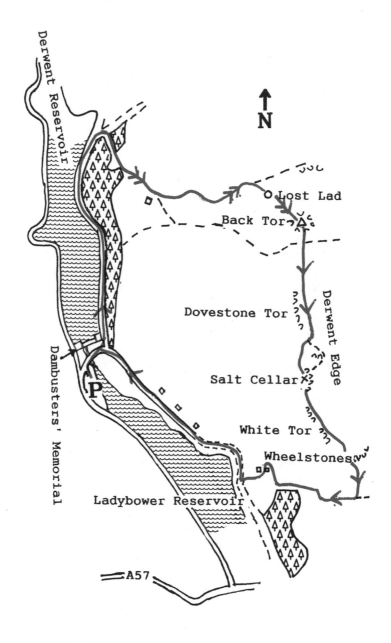

Derwent Reservoir

Dambusters' Memorial

N

O Lost Lad

Back Tor

Dovestone Tor

Derwent Edge

Salt Cellar

White Tor

Wheelstones

P

Ladybower Reservoir

A57

Walk 40

farm track and turn left. When track bends right by signpost, fork left down to stile and A57.

Cross and continue on far side to footbridge, turning left on track beyond. Turn left on farm access road but fork right after 200m/220yd at point (b). After 2.5km/1.6ml turn left at signpost for Derwent via Haggs. Track leads down to A57, doubling back before gate and then crossing river. Cross road and go up access road to Hagg Farm Centre, keeping straight on where road bends left. Track leads steeply up to corner of plantation at point (a) on ridge. Turn right and retrace outward route to carpark.

This walk could be shortened by going NW on stony track at point (a). Descend by Rowlee Farm, cross A57 and continue on farm road opposite. At sharp bend to right – point (b) – turn left on track uphill to pick up the main route. Save 4km/2.5ml.

40. Derwent Edge

Ordnance Survey Map No: 110 or OL No 1
Distance from city centre: 112km/70ml
Walking distance: 12.8km/8ml
Amount of climbing: 315m/1043ft

This popular route begins and ends with peaceful stretches among the trees by the reservoir and has as its centrepiece a dramatic walk along one of the Peak District's famous edges with many weatherworn out-crops and splendid views all round.

Park in Fairholmes carpark at N end of Ladybower Reservoir. SK172893. To get there take M62/M6/M56 (Stockport) and M66/M67/A57 (Sheffield) through Glossop. After 21km/13ml, just before viaduct, turn left at signpost for Derwent Valley. Carpark on right after 4km/2.5ml.

Walk past kiosk in carpark and take footpath on right to road. Turn right and cross bridge. Where road curves right take path on left leading to right-hand end of reservoir and joining stony track. Walk with reservoir on left to second footpath sign on right 2.5km/

1.6ml (just past bench on left). Fork right after 35m/ 40yd and leave plantation through gap in wall to follow path SE uphill on embankment. At corner of wood turn left with broken wall on right.

When wall bends right before ruins, fork left uphill on clear track. At signpost turn left with broken wall on left and at waymark turn right with wall still on left. Cross ladder stile to left and follow footpath sign for Strines to E on broad green track over level ground. After right-hand bend take right fork to panorama table on summit of Lost Lad.

Continue SE on paved path to TP on Back Tor. Path turns S along escarpment on right (boggy sections here soon to be paved). Pass series of weatherworn outcrops for 3.2km/2ml. After Wheelstones (also called Coach and Horses) ground drops to signpost by shooting butt. Turn right. (Short section not on OL map but route very clear.)

Walk 36   Wainstones – 'the Kiss'

Walk 37   Shining Tor from Cat's Tor

When path reaches wall turn right and then go left through gateway to corner of wood. Path follows plantation with wall on left and then right and passes through ruined farm with 17th-century barn down to Ladybower Reservoir. Turn right on rough track which becomes metalled and leads to carpark.

This walk can be shortened by turning right at signpost just after Back Tor. Path leads down to track by reservoir. Turn left for carpark. Save 2.5km/1.6ml.

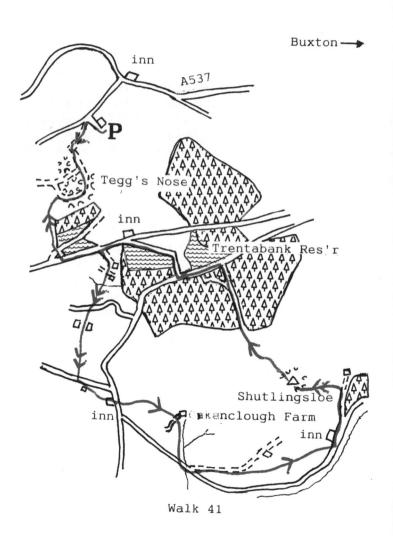

Buxton →

N

inn

A537

P

Tegg's Nose

inn

Trentabank Res'r

Shutlingsloe

inn   Oakenclough Farm

inn

Walk 41

41. Tegg's Nose and Shutlingsloe

Ordnance Survey Map No: 118 or OL No 24
Distance from city centre: 72km/45ml
Walking distance: 16km/10ml
Amount of climbing: 381m/1257ft

This most shapely peak has the somewhat exaggerated popular name of the Cheshire Matterhorn. The approach takes in steadily rising pastureland and a descent through a lovely little valley to reach the S side of the peak. A short climb to the summit is followed by a descent of the popular route over moorland and through forests and back by the side of some reservoirs.

Park at the Information Centre in Tegg's Nose Country Park E of Macclesfield. SJ950732. To get there take M62/M6 to J19, A5033 to Knutsford and A537 to Macclesfield. Follow signs to Buxton. After 1.6km/1ml from town centre take right-hand fork signposted for Tegg's Nose. Carpark on right after further 1.6km/1ml.

From carpark return to road and turn left by entrance on stony track signposted for Croker Hill. Follow Gritstone Trail markers (yellow bootprint with superimposed G) which lead past display of quarry machinery. Where track bends right keep ahead on smaller path and join track curving right. Cross waymarked stile on left and follow path down to reservoir. Cross embankment, lane and next embankment to lane beyond. Turn left and at end of reservoir go right on farm road signposted for Croker Hill.

Take left-hand fork to Throstle Farm and at farm entrance follow path to right of fence. Beyond stile turn left up stony track. Turn right through gate by barn on right and cross stiles, following hedge on left to reach stream, beyond which stiles lead to lane. Cross and continue to clearly waymarked route through complex of buildings. Continue through fields to next lane, last stile beyond stream being slightly to right. Turn left, leaving Gritstone Trail.

Turn up stone steps past house on right and follow track to Hanging Gate Inn. Cross lane to path opposite between fences. At stile turn right and go through gateway on right to continue with wall on left and then on green track with Shutlingsloe directly ahead. Pass pool on right and drop to Oakenclough Farm. Cross farm track and stile opposite, then go through gateway on left to go down valley with stream on right. At lane by Greenaway Bridge turn left and fork left in 100m/ 110yd on to farm access road.

At sharp bend on left, just before cattle grid, go over stile on right and follow waymarked route E. Cross stream and ladder stile. Series of marked stiles leads gradually down to lane on right by Crag Inn. Turn left and after 150m/165yd turn up farm lane on left. Route to summit is waymarked. From summit follow newly laid (1992) flagged path down to forest. Go through stile and turn right to signpost on track nearby. Turn left and follow track down to Trentabank Reservoir. Turn left to pass toilets and Information Centre. Keep right at junction, following signpost for Langley. Turn left by Leather's Smithy Inn to reach Bottoms Reservoir and outward route.

This route could be shortened by using the Forestry Commission carpark at Trentabank. SJ964711. Follow directions above from Trentabank to pick up main route and turn left on farm road signposted for Croker Hill. Save 5.6km/3.5ml.

Walk 42   Below the Roaches

Walk 42   The Roaches

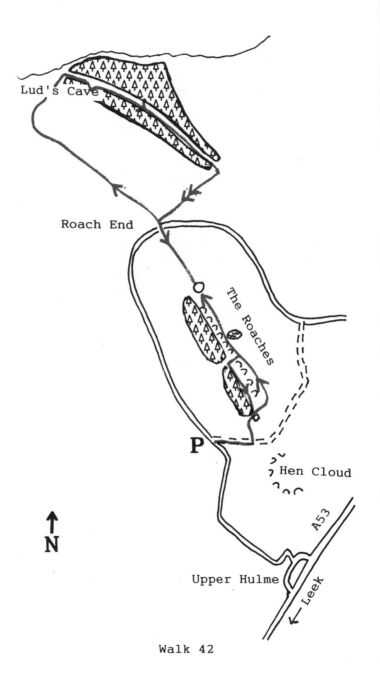

Lud's Cave

Roach End

The Roaches

P

Hen Cloud

A53

N

Upper Hulme

Leek

Walk 42

42. The Roaches

Ordnance Survey Map No: 118 and 119 or OL No 24
Distance from city centre: 102km/64ml
Walking distance: 11.5km/7ml
Amount of climbing: 361m/1191ft

The Roaches Estate is a delightful area to walk in and the ridge has wide views. Nearer at hand the crags are festooned with colourful ropes and covered with even more colourful rock climbers. Lud's Church was a place of worship for the Lollards.

Park at the foot of the crags on a minor road NW of Leek. Plenty of room but arrive early to be near col between Hen Cloud and the Roaches. SK004621. To get there use the M6/M62 to J17, A534 to Congleton, A54/A523 to Leek and A53 (Buxton). Turn left into village of Upper Hulme 5km/3ml from centre of Leek. Pass hill of Hen Cloud on right and park as near as possible to gate leading to col.

Go through gate on to track going half-right. Near crags follow signpost on left past cottage. Turn right up rock steps to ridge and turn left. Follow ridge, passing gully, pool and TP down to lane (Roach End). Cross lane, go over two stiles and continue NW with wall on left for 2km/1.25ml as far as junction with another path. Turn right with wall on left going N and then NE in direction of Gradbach. After 1km/0.6ml take fork on right signposted Lud's Church and watch for huge cleft in rocks on right, this is Lud's Church (notice on rock face). Return to path and continue through wood, following signs back to Roach End.

Cross road to retrace steps over summit of Roaches and past pool. Continue for 320m/300yd to reach gully. Climb down rocks on right in gully and then turn left and walk along base of crags until reaching track leading to lane. Turn right back to car parking.

This walk can be shortened by leaving out the circuit to Lud's Church and returning along the lane from Roach End. Save 5km/3ml.

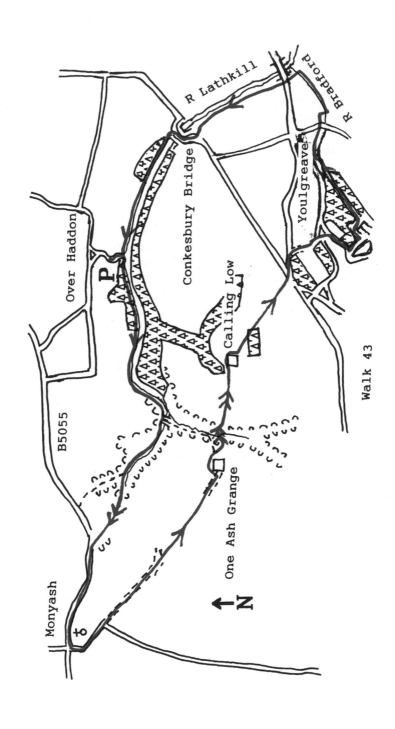

R Lathkill

R Bradford

Conkesbury Bridge

Over Haddon

P

Calling Low

Youlgreave

B5055

Monyash

One Ash Grange

N

Walk 43

43. *Lathkilldale*

Ordnance Survey Map No: 119 or OL No 24
Distance from city centre: 104km/65ml
Walking distance: 19.2km/12ml
Amount of climbing: 275m/908ft

This dale is so deep as to be scarcely visible from outside and with Bradford Dale, which completes the circuit, provides an absorbing day out among the hills if not actually on them.

Park opposite the chapel in Over Haddon. SK203664. To get there take M62/M6 to J19, A556/A5033/A537 to Knutsford and Macclesfield and A537/A54 to Buxton. Take road to Ashbourne, A515, and turn left on B5055 to Bakewell, turning on to second minor road on right past Monyash. This leads to Over Haddon. Carpark is down side street on right.

From carpark go down to river, turn right and walk up dale with river on left for 10km/6ml, passing bridge to Cales Dale on left and footpath on right up a side valley. On reaching B5055, turn left to Monyash and left at crossroads. When lane turns sharp right go ahead on track to One Ash Grange Farm and Cales Dale. Go through farm buildings, down into dale and up steep bank opposite, making for Calling Low Farm. Go through small wood and follow path SE to lane.

Cross lane and fork right to pass through picnic area. Follow Limestone Way markers down to lane, turn left and once past bend take path on right down to next lane. Turn right and when lane makes sharp bend to left take path on left through trees down to R. Bradford. Cross and turn left.

By Youlgreave it is necessary to cross to far bank before continuing to right downstream. When path reaches lane, go over but do not cross river by this bridge. Instead cross a little further on and continue with river on left to next bridge which takes path up to lane. Turn right, cross lane and continue with river on right to next lane. Turn right and cross Conkesbury Bridge. Turn left through gate immediately over

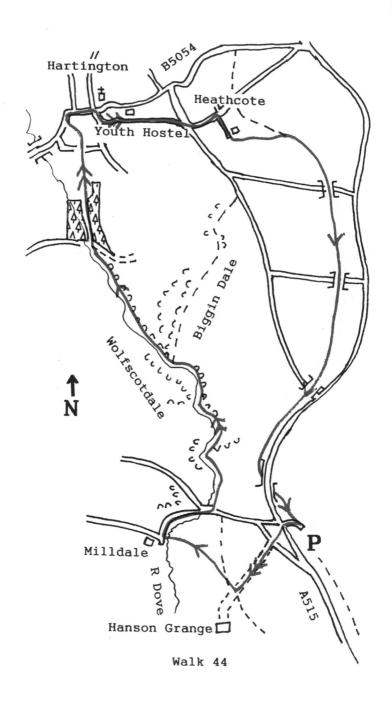

Hartington

B5054

Heathcote

Youth Hostel

Biggin Dale

Wolfscotdale

N

Milldale

R Dove

Hanson Grange

P

A515

Walk 44

bridge. The lane to Over Haddon is on the right after 1.5km/0.75ml.

It is possible to shorten this walk by turning left on lane after passing Calling Low Farm. This leads direct to Conkesbury Bridge. Save 2.3km/1.5ml.

44. *Tissington Trail and Wolfscotdale*

Ordnance Survey Map No: 119 or OL No 24
Distance from city centre: 112km/70ml
Walking distance: 18.5km/11.5ml
Amount of climbing: 230m/760ft

Another charming route by the rivers of the Derbyshire Dales with lovely views as far as Axe Edge from the Tissington Trail, a disused railway line.

Park at the former Alsop station just off the A515. SK156584. To get there take M62/M6 to J19 and A556/A5033/A537 to Knutsford and Macclesfield. Take Ashbourne road A515. Parking is on left after 24km/15ml.

Cross A515 and go over stile to reach lane on other side of field. Go along farm track opposite and, on reaching junction of paths after 0.8km/0.5ml, take footpath on right with wall on left down to Viator's Bridge and Milldale. Turn right on lane, cross river again after 1.5km/0.9ml and cross stile on left on other side of bridge to reach Wolfscotdale. Stay in dale as river winds among cliffs for 5km/3ml, passing exit on right by Biggin Dale. Path rises at far end of a wood to cross fields and enclosed lane by stiles to road at Hartington. Route is fully waymarked.

Turn right on road and right in village centre. At war memorial turn right and go up steep hill past Youth Hostel to Heathcote. Turn right in village centre and, past last farm on left, take footpath on left signposted for Friden. This goes almost E over stiles towards gates giving access to Tissington Trail. Turn right and follow trail for 6.4km/4ml to carpark.

This walk can be shortened by turning right up Biggin Dale to reach Heathcote. Save 4.0km/2.5ml.

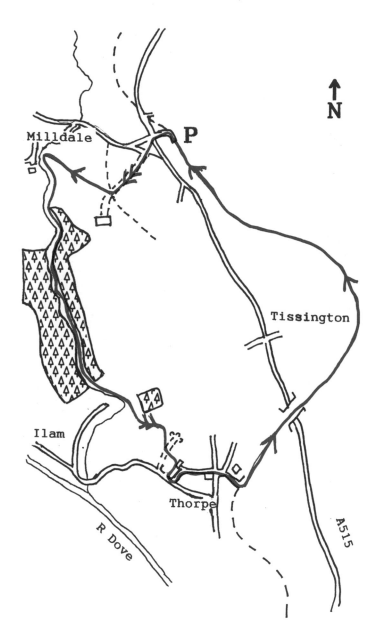

Milldale

P

N

Tissington

A515

Ilam

Thorpe

R Dove

Walk 45

45. *Tissington Trail and Dovedale*

Ordnance Survey Map No: 119 or OL No 24
Distance from city centre: 112km/70ml
Walking distance: 15.25km/9.5ml
Amount of climbing: 120m/360ft

This walk is a continuation of No 44 following the R. Dove in its better known stretches and the Tissington Trail. Popularisation by Izaac Walton has done nothing to diminish its beauty, but it is best kept in reserve for less-crowded days.

Park at the former Alsop station just off the A515. SK156584. To get there take M62/M6 to J19 and A556/A5033/A537 to Knutsford and Macclesfield. Take Ashbourne road A515. Parking is on left after 24km/15ml.

Cross A515 and go over stile to reach lane on other side of field. Go along farm track opposite. On reaching junction of paths after 0.8km/0.5ml, take footpath on right with wall to left down to Viator's Bridge. Do not cross but turn left and follow R. Dove downstream for 4.5km/2.6ml.

Just before stepping stones, cross stile and then gate on left to go up Lindale. Path curves right with small hill on left, then curves left and crosses a track to a wall on right. Go over stile in wall on right and cross fields to road.

Turn left and then at crossroads with Dog and Partridge on corner, go straight across to reach site of former railway station on Tissington Trail. Turn left and follow trail for 7km/4.25ml back to carpark at Alsop.

It is not practicable to shorten this walk.

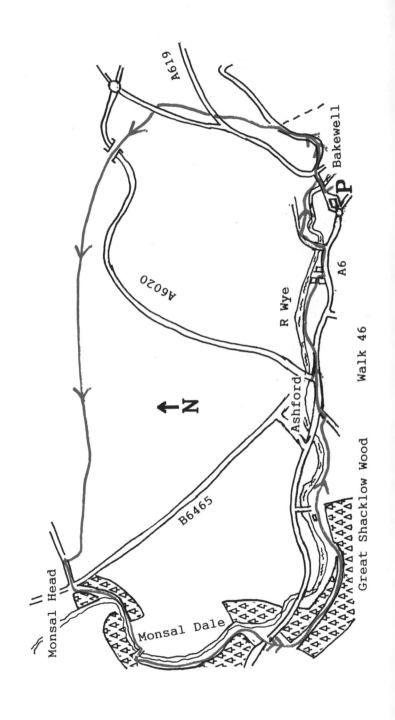

46. *Monsal Head*

Ordnance Survey Map No: 119 or OL No 24
Distance from city centre: 107km/67ml
Walking distance: 14.5km/9ml
Amount of climbing: 150m/495ft

Monsal Head is a magnificent viewpoint, while Monsal Dale is extremely picturesque. The walk continues through the lovely Great Shacklow Wood and passes the much-photographed Sheepwash Bridge at Ashford in the Water.

Park in the public carpark in Bakewell. SK229684. To get there take the M62/M6 to J19, A556/A5033/ A537 to Knutsford and Macclesfield, A537/A54 to Buxton and A6 to Bakewell. Turn left at roundabout into town and right into carpark. Further parking across bridge.

From carpark return to main street, turn right and cross road bridge over river, forking right and passing minor road on right to go uphill to site of former railway station. Turn left to join Monsal Trail, which follows old railway line. The line comes to an end after 5km/3ml at the end of a cutting. Take path on right to a lane and turn left to B6465 at Monsal Head.

Go right of the inn and cafe and over stile. Path descends steeply to left into Monsal Dale. Follow river, crossing bridge to continue on far side to A6. Cross road to carpark, bearing left to stile. Cross and follow footpath waymarked No 3, which goes uphill and left into Great Shacklow Wood by stile in wall. Footpath drops to Sheldon Mill and follows river to lane.

Turn left, cross A6 and turn right. From here it is 3.4km/2ml into Bakewell, but road walking can be avoided in part by looking for path on left which follows river bank before crossing lane between houses and rejoining A6. More road can be avoided by crossing packhorse bridge after a further 1km/0.5ml and continuing on far bank by lane and then riverside path into Bakewell.

It is not practicable to shorten this walk.

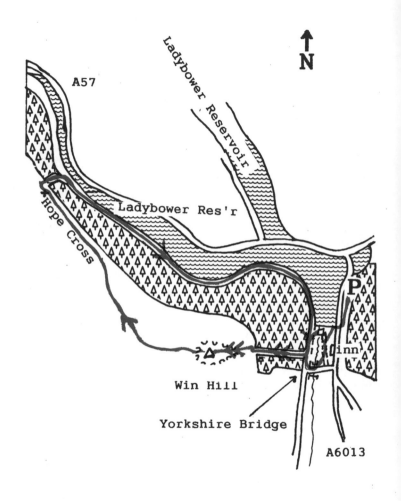

Walk 47

47. Win Hill

Ordnance Survey Map No: 110 or OL No 1
Distance from city centre: 110km/69ml
Walking distance: 14.5km/9ml
Amount of climbing: 382m/1260ft
An initial very steep climb is followed by a fine ridge with views of Kinder Scout and the Lose Hill ridge. After a descent through woodland a tranquil track leads along the edge of Ladybower Reservoir. (Note that the very start of the walk is not on OL map.)

Park in Heatherdene carpark off A6013 on E side of Ladybower Reservoir. SK202859. To get there take M62/M6/M56 (Stockport) and M66/M67/A57 (Sheffield) through Glossop. Turn right at junction with A6013. Carpark on left just after end of viaduct.

Follow sign for picnic area and toilets at S end of carpark and when level with dam descend steps on right, cross road and go down signposted footpath. At junction with track turn left and, just before gate, fork right to stile on lane. Turn right, cross Yorkshire Bridge, turn right again and go up steep steps on left. Cross track and stile and follow path uphill by stream on left.

Continue up steps after crossing another track and leave plantation by stile slightly to left. Turn right and immediately left to maintain direction uphill through trees and on to open moorland. Cross ladder stile to reach TP on rocky knoll.

Broad track continues W. Fork right to reach signpost and continue in direction of Hope Cross. After short section with wall on left and fence on right, track curves gradually right and drops to continue with plantation on right. When main track curves away to left keep by trees and cross stile to walk between wall on left and plantation on right to reach Hope Cross, a 3m/10ft column with square cap, dated 1737.

Cross stile and turn right into wood through small gate. At ruins do not take turning to right but keep ahead. Turn right on track at foot of hill and right again a few m/yd beyond. Follow this forestry track for 5km/3ml with reservoir on left, back to Yorkshire Bridge. Turn left to retrace outward route.

This walk can be shortened by turning right on track into woods at the point where main route from summit reaches edge of plantation. This leads down to track by reservoir. Turn right for Yorkshire Bridge. Save 3km/1.9ml.

Walk 56 Cracoe Obelisk (war memorial)

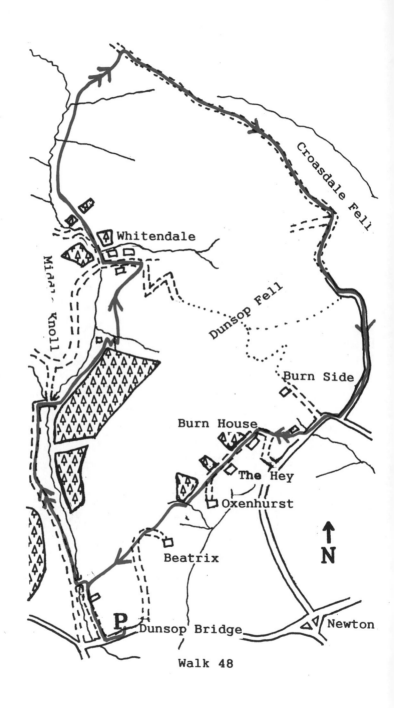

Croasdale Fell

Whitendale

Wiaar Knoll

Dunsop Fell

Burn Side

Burn House

The Hey

Oxenhurst

Beatrix

P

Dunsop Bridge

Newton

N

Walk 48

BOWLAND AND RIBBLE VALLEY

48. Croasdale Fell

Ordnance Survey Map No: 103
Distance from city centre: 104km/65ml
Walking distance: 20.8km/13ml
Amount of climbing: 376m/1241ft

Although some of the old tracks to the hill farms have been surfaced and there is some walking on quiet lanes, this remains one of my favourite walks in this area at any season. Beyond Whitendale it is particularly lonely and the air is filled with the cries of larks, lapwings and curlews.

Park in Dunsop Bridge. SD661502. To get there take M62/M6 to J32 and A6 to Broughton. Turn right at traffic lights on B5269 to Longridge. At roundabout turn left on minor road and follow signposts for Whitewell, Trough of Bowland and Dunsop Bridge. At Dunsop Bridge turn right over bridge. Carpark is on left past garage.

From carpark turn right and just before bridge turn right on access road. Go past cottages, through gate, turn left over bridge and right on access road. After 2.9km/1.6ml turn right over two bridges and continue NE with stream on left. (Some of this road walking can be avoided by keeping near stream or walking on flood embankment on right.)

On reaching small stone hut go up zigzag track on right – track starts by tree on right and goes S initially. Now cross two bridges and stay on high-level track to Whitendale Farm. Go left between walls and past barns to access road. Turn right and go through gate to left of farmhouse. When track forks keep right and go uphill between two young plantations. Path becomes fainter but keep stream to left until valley turns left. Then go straight uphill to join Roman road. There are some marker posts, not easy to find, but any line uphill will reach the track. Turn right and follow this track downhill. The track becomes a lane and joins another where you turn right. 1.3km/0.75ml past a sharp left-hand bend the road drops. On left is a small disused quarry and to right a gate leading to barn in field. Go through gate, passing barn on right to field corner and continue with wall on left to access road to Burn House. Turn right and follow road past farm on left. Keep on track SW, passing The Hey on left and wood on right. Just before track swings left and down to Oxenhurst go through gate in front and keep hedge on left. Follow waymarkers by wood on right down to stream. Cross and go up steep bank opposite with stream on right. At top continue with fence on right, over stiles to Beatrix Farm. Turn right on access road and go through gate on right just past wall. Follow line of telephone poles across field (no visible path) and by last pole turn slightly left to stile in wall. Go down steep bank to track, turn left and retrace outward route to carpark.

This walk can be shortened by turning right up a track on reaching Whitendale Farm. Follow marker posts to gate in wall on top of Dunsop Fell where track divides. Do not take left-hand track with posts, but turn right by wall for 200m/220yd until faint path goes left away from wall. Once over very boggy patch this becomes a good track leading down spur, past Burn Side (Alsatians) to lane. Turn right to join main route. A good walk in its own right, this saves 6.4km/4ml.

Walk 48   Dunsop Fell

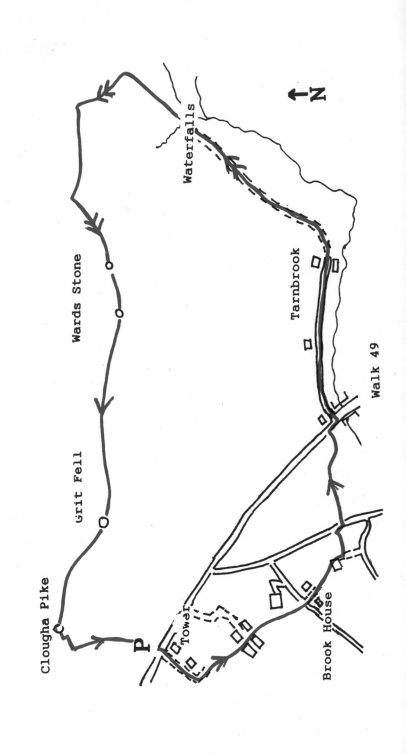

49. Ward's Stone

Ordnance Survey Map No: 102
Distance from city centre: 122km/76ml
Walking distance: 22.5km/14ml
Amount of climbing: 521m/1719ft

Most of this walk is on areas with access agreements and for half its length is on a narrow strip which must not be left. As this is one of the best bits, it is not likely that you will be remotely tempted!

Park opposite the Jubilee Tower on the Trough of Bowland road. SD542574. To get there take the M62/M6 to J34 and A683 (Sedbergh). Before Caton turn right on minor road signposted Trough of Bowland and follow signs for 11km/6.75ml. Tower is on right, carpark on left.

Cross road from carpark and go down access road to right of tower to Westfield House. Follow track through farm buildings. Track takes sharp turn left, going almost due S. Past Lee Tenement it becomes a path and can be followed across fields by keeping in same direction and picking up series of gates and stiles. It leads through Low Moor Head Farm, over a minor road and along the access road to Brook House (old school and graveyard). From here go over footbridge to Chapel House Farm. Beyond farm buildings take path on left to lane, turn right and, after 200m/220yd, take footpath on left to reach lane. Turn right and take lane on left before crossing the main river. If all this is too much, turn left from the carpark and walk down the road for 3.5km/2ml to reach the same point more tediously!

Follow lane with river on right to houses at end and go through on to track to waterfalls, by which time track is a path. Posts and cairns lead NE on to broad ridge where route follows fence NW and then W almost as far as TP on summit of Ward's Stone. A second TP is situated 600m/660yd SW.

Keep on high ground for 3.2km/2ml on cairned path W to Grit Fell. From here it is 1.5km/0.8ml NW to the

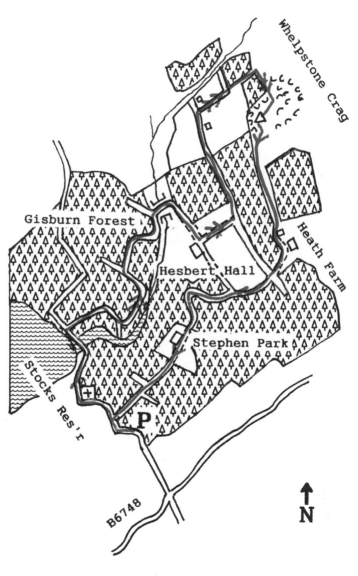

Walk 50

TP on Clougha Pike. To reach carpark, go SE down rake across crags, cross the stream and then head S to stile in fence and tower.

This walk may be shortened by descending from Grit Fell, following fence to carpark. Save 2km/1.25ml.

50. Whelpstone Crag

Ordnance Survey Map No: 103
Distance from city centre: 114km/71ml
Walking distance: 15km/9ml
Amount of climbing: 221m/729ft

For the most part this route follows forestry tracks since the rights of way have been planted over, leaving almost no trace. Recent felling, however, has opened up the area which is very quiet. Views from the little summit are extensive through 360 degrees and it is an absorbing exercise to take some maps and identify distant peaks. In winter Stocks Reservoir is worth a visit to see migrant birds.

Park in small picnic site E of Slaidburn. SD745550. To get there take M62/M6 to J31 and A59 to Clitheroe. Take B6478 to Waddington, Newton and Slaidburn, then follow signs for Settle. Turn left at crossroads at brown tourist sign to Gisburn Forest 5km/3ml E of Slaidburn. Carpark on right after 400m/0.25ml by sign for Bowland Forest.

Turn right on lane, pass church on right, cross end of reservoir and turn right on forestry track. Pass small track on right and turn right on next track. Turn right downhill at next junction and cross bridge. Opposite farm buildings on right (Hesbert Hall) go through gate on left and up to forestry track. Turn left. In clear felled area look in restored barn on right for pegged-oak beams. Turn right on forestry track before next barn and pass remains of Clough Hall on left. Summit comes into view.

After sharp left turn go up right with plantation and wall on left and then through soggy fire break to stile. Cross and turn right. Go through gap by stone gatepost

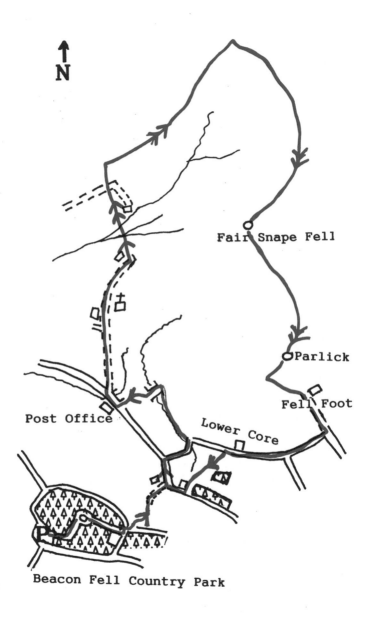

Fair Snape Fell

Parlick

Fell Foot

Post Office

Lower Core

Beacon Fell Country Park

Walk 51

to ascend between wall and fence. On top turn right for TP.

Descend SSE by wall on right – the ground is boggy and the track intermittent. Cross stile and walk through fire break (overtrousers recommended if grass wet). Cross stile and continue between wall and fence. At end of fence follow forest edge to stone stile in corner on right by gate and concrete building. Follow farm track between buildings and down to forestry track.

Turn right – SW – aiming for distant reservoir. At junction turn left. Pass Stephen Park Outdoor Centre, pass one turning on left and one on right and reach lane. Turn left to carpark.

It is possible to shorten this walk by continuing past Hesbert Hall and taking the next major turning on right, leading to Stephen Park. Save 5.5km/3.5ml.

51. *Fair Snape Fell and Parlick*

Ordnance Survey Map No: 102
Distance from city centre: 93km/58ml
Walking distance: 20km/12ml
Amount of climbing: 593m/1957ft

This walk begins with an approach through a quiet, pastoral landscape but then rises to cross boggy moorland followed by a superb ridge before dropping down to farmland again. Needs an early start.

Park at Fell House carpark in Beacon Fell Country Park. SD565426. To get there use the M62/M6 to J32. Take the A6(N) and after 1km/0.5ml turn right at the traffic lights in Broughton on the B5269. Turn left opposite a garage, following sign for Beacon Fell Country Park. From here the route is a maze of country lanes but every junction is clearly signposted. If Fell House is full there is ample parking around the fell road, but the walk instructions start from this point.

From carpark take cobbled track going E and after 200m/220yd, where tracks cross, go left uphill with wall on left to TP. Turn right (E) and descend to quarry carpark, continuing ahead to fell road. Turn left and almost immediately down lane on right.

Cross stile on left after 50m and go half-right down field to pick up track leading to gate and sunken farm track. Follow this track downhill, past farm on left to road. Turn left and then right at T-junction. At right-hand turn in road, cross stile on left and follow wall and then stream on left, crossing stream by stone slab. Follow fence on right to lane and turn right.

Pass Post Office, cross bridge and go up private road on right, taking left-hand fork towards small wood. Pass school on left and church on right, following lane all the way to farm at end.

Footpath on right is signposted by cattle-grid. Follow it round farm and uphill with fence on right, over three bridges until reaching stone track. Cross and go steeply up to stile in stone wall. Cross, go right and follow track up fellside until reaching wire fence on plateau.

Follow fence for 2km/1.25ml, passing cairn on left on highest point of fell and stile to Wolf Fell Access Area.

When fence curves S, continue W to reach TP, cairn and shelter on rim of plateau in five minutes. A cairned track leads SE down and up again to Parlick, meeting wall on left. At end of wall follow fence to summit of Parlick. Follow fence down until meeting stile and take path on left down to Fell Foot.

Go down access road to lane and turn right. Continue in same direction on joining another lane. Opposite Lower Core Farm (D 1897 over door) just past steps on left, go through gate on left and cross field to next lane, keeping wood on left and aiming for right-hand end of second wood. Turn right and where lane turns right go up farm track on left. You have now joined the outward route and can retrace steps back to carpark.

Because much of this route lies in agreed access areas, it is not possible to shorten it.

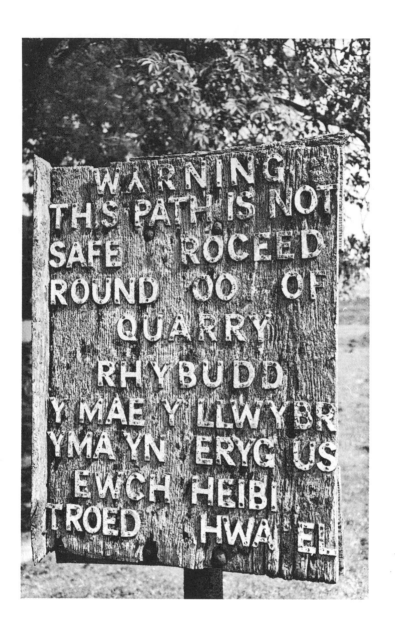

Walk 20   Well-worn and out of date!

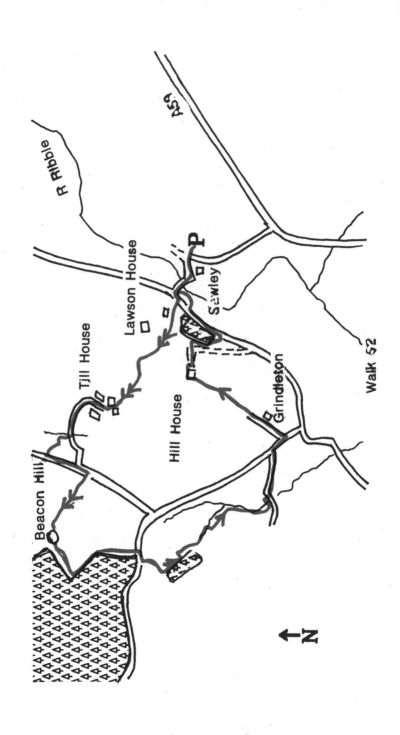

R Ribble

A59

Lawson House

P

Sawley

Till House

Lawson House

Hill House

Grindleton

Beacon Mill

Walk 52

← N

52. Beacon Hill

Ordnance Survey Map No: 103
Distance from city centre: 101km/63ml
Walking distance: 10km/6.3ml
Amount of climbing: 275m/907ft

A short walk with plenty of variety and good views from a modest summit.

Park with permission at the Sawley Arms. SD776464. To get there take the M62/M6 to J31 and then the A59 past Clitheroe. The turning to Sawley is on left, 1km/0.6ml past the northerly turning to Chatburn. Carpark on right. Also limited roadside parking by riverbank.

Cross road to R. Ribble and turn left, downstream, to bridge. Cross, take left fork in road and after 70m/75yd go up lane on right, signposted Friends' Meeting House. Go to left of houses, up concrete ramp by garage and over stile. Go uphill following white markers keeping to hedge on left. Pass between two oaks at top of rise, drop down to stile and bridge and continue with hedge on left.

Near Till House go left of white building and through gate. Turn right and ahead on lane between farm buildings. By cattle-grid turn right through wicket gate, crossing stream and at next gate follow hedge on left to narrow stile and over rise to gate on lane.

Turn left and after 200m/220yd go through gate on right just past covered reservoir and follow path on top of embankment to stile. Summit of Beacon Fell is visible 100m/110yd to SSW. To regain track go W to stone wall at edge of felled plantation, turn left and descend between walls, over stile to gate where track turns right and wall turns SE. Turn left to follow this wall just inside edge of plantation; right of way leads to fell road.

Turn right for 20m/22yd and go left through second of two gates down to a thin strip of wood. Turn uphill with wood on right to stone wall and go left to stile. Cross and go ESE downhill by stiles and gates to meet stream and hedge which are kept to right as you

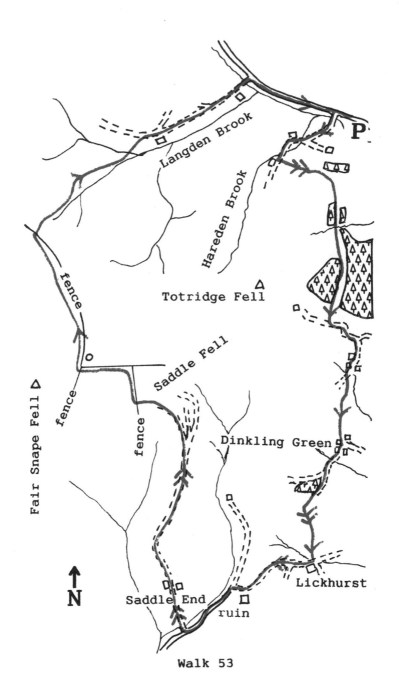

Langden Brook

Hareden Brook

P

△ Totridge Fell

Saddle Fell

Fair Snape Fell △

fence

fence

fence

Dinkling Green

N

Saddle End

ruin

Lickhurst

Walk 53

descend. Go through gate right and continue downhill with hedge now left to stream at bottom of field. Turn right, following stream and crossing near lane to stile in field corner on left. Go uphill on lane, turn right at junction and descend to Grindleton.

At sign to Methodist Church turn left and continue at lane end into fields with hedge on left, past small barn and then with wire fence on right to Hill House Farm. Go through farmyard and when access road turns right keep ahead over stile to wood. Turn right at edge of wood to gate and track down to road. Turn left and after 300m go right to riverbank at Ribble Way sign. This leads back to bridge and Sawley Arms.

To shorten this walk continue downhill on the fell road past the reservoir. This leads directly to Grindleton. Save 1km/0.75ml.

53. Saddle Fell

Ordnance Survey Map No: 103
Distance from city centre: 107km/67ml
Walking distance: 21km/13ml
Amount of climbing: 670m/2211ft

This is an exacting walk because it is seldom possible to set a good pace. The first section is an enjoyable ramble through pastureland, though lack of signposting keeps you alert. This is followed by a climb on a good track to boggy uplands and an exhilarating high-level path, dropping down to a long, stony track.

Parking area on W side of Trough of Bowland road, 1.66km/1ml N of Dunsop Bridge. SD646506. To get there take M62/M6 to J32 and A6 to Broughton. Turn right at traffic lights on B5269 to Longridge. At roundabout turn left on minor road and follow tourist signs for Trough of Bowland. Pass turning to Dunsop Bridge on right. Parking area on left beyond cattle-grid.

From carpark go NW on road and after 250m/275yd cross bridge on left on access road. Cross bridge on right and past second bridge go over stile on left. Keep on centre of ridge and gradually climb to right to gate and stile at junction of walls. Continue on track ahead and then turn right at yellow marker post. Follow tractor marks for easiest route to ladder stile to left of gate ahead. Continue SW towards wood. Meet wall on left and go through small gate. After 20m/22yd fork right at end of low wall by marker post. Path crosses stream and contours hill, passing between wall on left and fence on right before entering plantation. Avoid very muddy section by going through trees on left. Past plantation turn left on metalled lane and right at junction. Path goes between farm buildings on right and crosses bridge by ford. Turn left to follow stream and after 100m/110yd watch for section of fence right with no barbed wire which is where right of way crosses. Cross stile to right of gate and on far side of field go under single strand of plain wire and through gate between farm buildings. Go through gate on right on to rough track crossing stream. At fork go left. Past gate walk with fence on right, go through gate ahead and gate on left, with fence again to right.

Pass between stone gateposts and gate half-right beyond. Make for Lickhurst Farm ahead, crossing two stiles before dropping down to access road. Turn right, cross bridge, pass farmhouse on left and go through gate ahead on to stony track. At left-hand bend keep ahead on track through gate. At top of rise, where several tracks split off, keep to main, sunken track. After 0.8km/0.5ml ford stream and just past ruin turn left on lane.

After 1.2km/0.75ml turn right up concrete access road to Saddle End Farm. Pass farm buildings, go through gate and follow signposted track to Saddle Fell. Where track divides keep left to join fence and cross stile. Turn right following fence and at fence junction turn left still with fence right to ladder stile. Cross and turn right, passing cairn and post marking summit of fell.

After 1.6km/1ml cross ladder stile on right and join cairned path beyond boggy patch. At bottom of valley ford stream as indicated by marker posts and join stony track leading to Trough of Bowland road. Turn right for carpark.

Because of limited access it is not possible to shorten this walk. A worthwhile alternative would be to walk NW on road to Langden Brook and follow valley path to the ladder stile returning by same route. Save 14km/ 8.75ml.

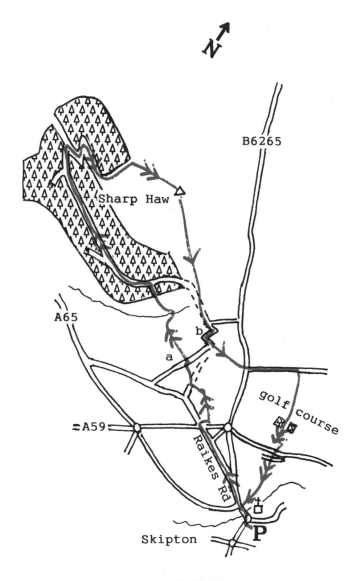

N

B6265

Sharp Haw

A65

b

a

golf course

A59

Raikes Rd

Skipton

P

Walk 54

THE YORKSHIRE DALES

54. Sharp Haw

Ordnance Survey Map No: 103 or OL No 10
Distance from city centre: 123km/77ml
Walking distance: 12km/7.5ml
Amount of climbing: 340m/1120ft

A very satisfying short walk which, with an early start, can be combined with a visit to the castle or the market in Skipton. Pronounced locally "Sharper", the elegant shape of the summit is in view for most of the time.

Park in Skipton. SD991518. To get there use M62/M6 to J31 and A59 to Skipton. Carpark on right at N end of High Street.

Return to High Street, cross and turn right. Follow road curving left and cross canal. Fork right on Raikes Road. Fork left again on Raikes Road and stay on it crossing bridge over bypass. Follow waymarks to right leading to footpath above bypass and then cross stile on left into fields.

When fence turns sharp left go half right to next fence corner and then downhill to stile by gate half-right. Cross and go right to stile by caravan park leading to lane. Turn right. At top end of caravan site pass through kissing gate on left and go half-right to stile on lane. Turn right and cross next stile (signposted for Flasby). Keep to left edge of field over two stiles and then stone stile by gate. Stone wall now on right. Past next stile walk on embankment and detour to right to easier crossing of stream. Make for gate left of rear of box van and turn left on forest track.

After 0.5km/0.3ml take right fork. When track curves sharply left keep ahead on path through rhododendrons at signpost for Flasby. Cross clearing and turn right on track going uphill by zigzags to fence. Cross and curve left to follow wall left. When this turns left, go uphill to right on improving ridge path to TP on summit.

Descent is over stile and down grassy path SE with some marker posts. Past gate path is less clear but maintain direction down to track. Turn left and follow down to lane. Keep straight ahead and at second right-hand bend cross stile to keep SE by broken fence on right over stiles to B6265. Cross and go down lane opposite.

On bend turn right to follow waymarked path through fields to golf course. Marker posts indicate route through trees to small hill in front. Turn left to find stile and go downhill half right to stile on bypass. *Cross with extreme caution as traffic is fast-moving.*

Cross stiles ahead which lead over brow of hill, down to lane and to Raikes Road. Turn left for carpark.

This walk may be shortened by parking at point (b) and walking along lane to pick up route at point (a). Save 5km/3ml.

Walk 56   Rylstone Cross to Cracoe Obelisk (war memorial)

Walk 57   The Swastika Stone

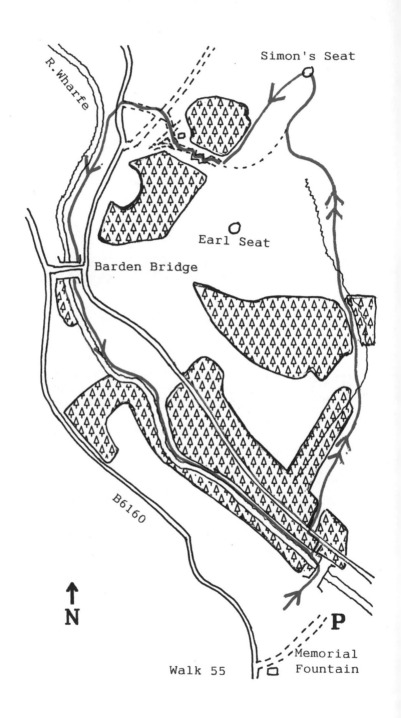

Simon's Seat

R.Wharfe

Earl Seat

Barden Bridge

B6160

N

P

Walk 55

Memorial
Fountain

55. *Simon's Seat*

Ordnance Survey Map No: 104 or OL No 10
Distance from city centre: 133km/83ml
Walking distance: 13.6km/8.5ml
Amount of climbing: 400m/1320ft

A walk full of variety: woods followed by moors, crags, more woods and, finally, a riverside.

Park at the Cavendish Pavilion NW of Bolton Abbey. SE078553. To get there take the M62/M6 to J31 and then the A59 (Clitheroe and Skipton) to Bolton Abbey. Turn left on the B6160 and right for the carpark by a large memorial fountain.

Cross the bridge over the R. Wharfe, turn left and go up steps to a lane and left on to the lane. Turn right at a cottage and follow a well defined track uphill with woods on left. Pass waterfall and enter wood to emerge on to moorland and follow prominent track N to Simon's Seat.

From summit go SW on track (signpost Howgill and Barden). Track meets wall and descends between walls through plantation. After 0.8km/0.5ml take track on right by barn (Signpost Howgill and Barden), cross lane (cafe 200m/0.2ml on right) and continue down to road. Cross and go half-left to river. Turn left and follow river bank as far as Barden Bridge. Cross road and continue by river through the woods until meeting the lane and bridge leading to the carpark.

It is possible to shorten this walk by turning left after coming out of the first wood and following its edge down to lanes leading to the river at Barden Bridge. Save 4.5km/3ml.

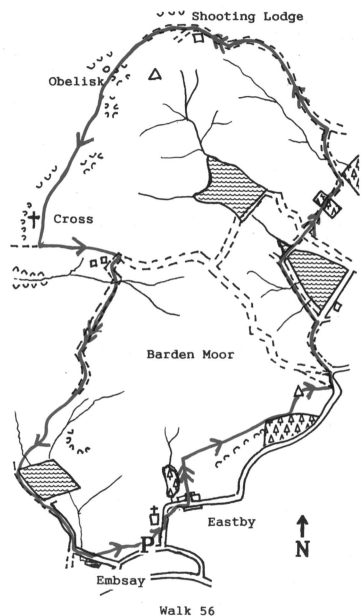

Shooting Lodge

Obelisk

Cross

Barden Moor

Eastby

↑
N

Embsay

P

Walk 56

56. Barden Moor

Ordnance Survey Map Nos: 98, 103 and 104 or OL 10
Distance from city centre: 126km/79ml
Walking distance: 21km/13ml
Amount of climbing: 580m/1900ft

A good leg-stretcher with little steep climbing, this walk makes a circuit of the moor by using an extensive network of tracks, well maintained for the use of shooting parties. There will certainly be closure of parts of the access areas from 12 August each year, so careful timing is needed if you want to enjoy the spectacular covering of heather in high summer. The OL map is recommended.

Park in Embsay village. SE009538. To get there, take M62/M6 to J31 and A59 to Skipton. At N end of High Street turn right at roundabout in front of Parish Church and after 0.7km/0.4ml turn left on minor road to Embsay. Carpark at far end of village on left.

Stile at back of carpark gives access to footpath going NE over stiles to lane. Turn left and cross lane at end of churchyard to regain footpath. At lane turn right into Eastby and left at footpath sign to Eastby Moor. Pass between houses on to track under trees. Once out of trees cross five stiles until reaching open moorland.

Turn right and follow wall on right until this starts to go down at far end of wood. Maintain height (no real path) to TP and keep in same direction down to lane below on right. Turn left and after crossing cattle-grid go left on metalled road towards reservoir. Turn left at sign to Upper Barden Reservoir and right again at similar sign to cross bridge at end of reservoir. Go up opposite bank and cross track on to another with wall on left going NNE.

Pass through small plantation and through gate in wall on left near mature plantation. Follow main track NW to shooting lodge conspicuous on skyline, ignoring several tracks going off to left. Fork right 50m/55yd past lodge and keep on track, now going W and curving SW to finish by wall.

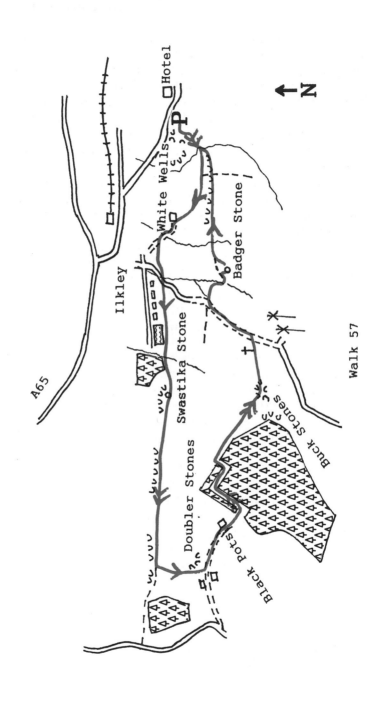

N

Hotel

White Wells

Ilkley

A65

Badger Stone

Swastika Stone

Doubler Stones

Buck Stones

Black Posts

Walk 57

Follow wall right, passing obelisk (Cracoe village war memorial) and then Rylstone Cross. Keep wall on right, now going S and SE until bridleway crosses wall by stone posts with blue markings. Turn left to follow bridleway, only a path but with wooden marker posts, until reaching another stony track by two shooting huts. Turn right and follow track S over brow of hill.

At top of hill, track becomes grass and then drops down to right-hand end of reservoir, becoming only a path through bracken. At track turn left. Track becomes metalled and bends left. Opposite mill pond on right go up stone steps on left by footpath sign and over seven stiles back to carpark.

It is not practicable to shorten this walk.

57. Ilkley Moor

Ordnance Survey Map No: 104
Distance from city centre: 136km/85ml
Walking distance: 15km/9.4ml
Amount of climbing: 240m/800ft

More properly called Rombald's Moor – it is the part called Ilkley Moor that we have all heard of. Away from the carparks and rock climbers above Ilkley, the moor is fairly quiet and offers spacious views as well as the chance to look at prehistoric rock carvings near the many ancient routes and burial mounds.

Park above Ilkley and below Cow and Calf Hotel. SE132467. To get there take M62/M6 to J31, A59/A677/A6119 (Blackburn), M65 to Colne and A6068 to Glusburn. Turn right on to A629 (Keighley), left on A6034 (Addingham) and right on A65 to Ilkley. Turn right at sign for Town Centre and Ilkley Moor. Pass railway station on left and turn right at sign for Cow and Calf Rocks. Carpark on right.

Walk W up stepped track but before reaching large, square quarry entrance, take stepped track on left to top of rise. Go SW on large track to crags half-right on skyline. When track forks go right to walk below crags on left (Rocky Valley). At valley-end join broader track from left leading down to left of conspicuous white building (White Wells). (Lower building is toilet block.) Follow broad stony track W. After railings on right take left fork contouring W through bracken. Go left at next fork, cross metalled lane and continue W with wall and houses on right. After passing reservoir on right do not go through kissing gate on right but continue to gap in corner of wall junction. Keep in same direction (no wall) making for iron railings on skyline ahead around Swastika Stone.

Continue W on path over stiles on edge of escarpment for 2.5km/1.5ml. Just past line of stone shooting butts on left look for yellow arrow on rock low on right and another on boulder on left. At this point turn left to slit stile in wall on left. Over stile follow path through heather to farm track and turn left. Note Doubler Stones on left.

Follow track SE and take waymarked bridleway to right of Black Pots Farm. Enter forest and turn left to follow path NE with wall/fence on left to corner of plantation and then SE to ladder stile. Cross and continue with wall on right. At bend leave wall and head for Buck Stones, prominent on skyline to right of TV masts. (In mist wall can be followed to ridge and then left.) Follow path, now broader, ESE to Cowper's Cross with TV masts on right. A few paces beyond Cross turn left on broad stony track. After 1.1km/0.5ml just before track turns left a track crosses where streams start and is marked on left by two short, thick posts. Turn right on track through bracken, soon becoming very broad. Contour head of spring. (To visit Badger Stone by seat take faint track right and return. Small swastika carving low on S side.) Continue on track over top of Rocky Valley, taking left fork and crossing track by large cairn. When Cow and Calf Hotel comes into sight track drops left towards square rear entrance to quarry. Skirt round quarry edge, turn left and carpark is in view. This walk could be shortened by retracing steps after viewing Swastika Stone. Save 7km/4.4ml.

Walk 70   Ruined windmill on Harrock Hill

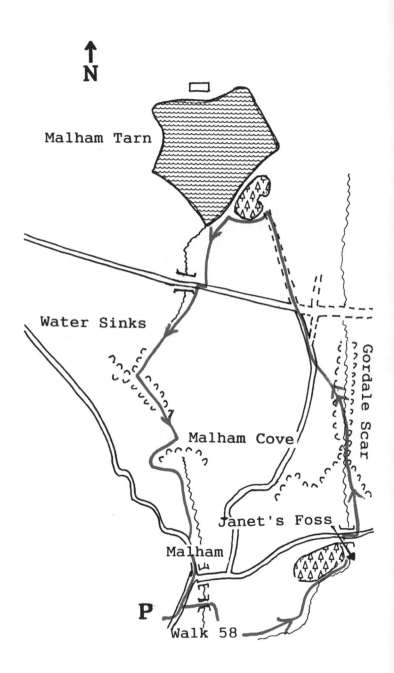

58. Malham Cove

Ordnance Survey Map No: 98 or OL 10
Distance from city centre: 139km/87ml
Walking distance: 10.25km/6.5ml
Amount of climbing: 190m/630ft

A classic walk which visits a number of spectacular geological features in beautiful countryside. Best not walked on Bank Holidays.

Public carpark at S edge of village. SD901627. To get there take the M62/M6 to J31. Turn right on to the A59 to Skipton and then the A65 towards Settle. Turn right at Gargrave and then left to Malham on minor roads (signposted Malham).

Turn left out of the carpark, right over a footbridge and right again to follow Gordale Beck on a well made path over a series of stiles across fields and then through a wood to Janet's Foss (a waterfall). The path goes left up to the lane. Turn right and then left through a gate signposted Gordale Scar.

Follow the path into the gorge to the waterfalls and look for the steep path to left (7m/20ft of scrambling). At the top go over a ladder stile (signpost Malham Tarn) and keep to a green path which bears left to a stile on to a lane. Turn right and when the lane turns left keep straight ahead, making for a wood. Turn left here to walk by the edge of the tarn and follow its outlet down to the lane. Turn right to cross the stream and then left through a gate. Keep to the stream bed even when the stream disappears underground, following the wall on the left into a dry valley all the way to the limestone pavement on the top of Malham Cove.

Turn right (signposts) along the top of the cove and follow the well made track over stiles down to the bottom of the cove and across fields by the beck. Signposts lead back to the village.

This walk can be shortened by turning left on the lane at the head of Gordale Scar and returning direct to Malham. Save 3km/1.75ml.

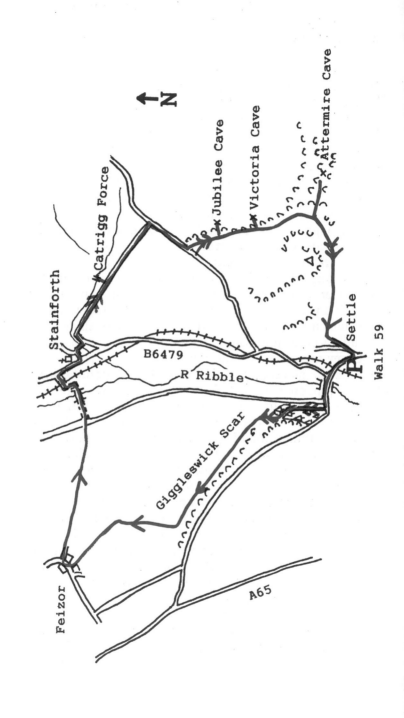

N

Catrigg Force

Jubilee Cave

Victoria Cave

Attermire Cave

Stainforth

B6479

R Ribble

Settle

Walk 59

Giggleswick Scar

Feizor

A65

59. Giggleswick Scar

Ordnance Survey Map No: 98 or OL No 2
Distance from city centre: 149km/93ml
Walking distance: 16km/10ml
Amount of climbing: 440/1450ft

A beautiful walk amongst limestone scenery on grassy paths for the most part, with waterfalls and several notable caves which can be explored if you take a powerful torch.

Park in public carpark near railway viaduct. SD819638. To get there take M62/M6 to J34, A683/A687 to Ingleton and A65 to Settle. Turn off on B6479 into town and cross river. Carpark is on right just after passing under railway viaduct.

From carpark cross road, turn left and go over river. When road turns right go up The Mains on right. Pass last house (Woodlands Guest House) and continue on track which curves left through trees to reach open ground. Follow footpath signs uphill and round edge of quarry on left.

Continue on edge of Giggleswick Scar until path nears main road on left. Go through gate in wall and then diagonally right to second gate following footpath signs to Feizor.

Turn right on lane and right on next track, signposted for Stainforth. This can be followed SE all the way down to the lane at Little Stainforth, the route being over stiles and through gates. Cross lane and go down to packhorse bridge over river. Cross and follow lane uphill, over railway and to B6479. Cross road and turn right.

Enter village by carpark on left, cross bridge on right in village and turn left parallel with stream to gain walled track going SE uphill. Catrigg Force on left is signposted by gate. Return after visit and cross stile. Continue on track SE to cattle-grid on lane. Turn right.

At next cattle-grid turn left at footpath sign and walk below limestone outcrops on left, keeping to higher tracks where possible and going up left to visit caves.

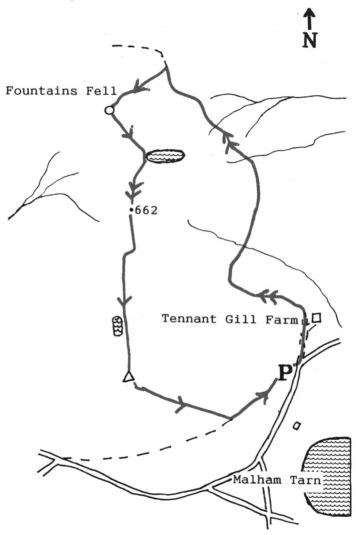

Pen y Ghent

Fountains Fell

N

•662

Tennant Gill Farm

P

Malham Tarn

Walk 60

For Attermire Cave, the longest, keep on a narrow high-level track where main track starts to drop to gate and climb easy rocks to higher terrace.

To continue walk, follow main track W with wall on left. Go half-right over low rise by small cave, continuing with wall on right until meeting cross wall and track. Turn left to descend into Settle.

Turn right at main road for carpark.

This walk may be shortened by turning right instead of crossing Stainforth Bridge. Follow river bank and Ribble Way signs into Settle. Save 3km/1.9ml.

60.   Fountains Fell

Ordnance Survey Map No: 98 or OL No 10
Distance from city centre: 136km/85ml
Walking distance: 10.4km/6.5ml
Amount of climbing: 295/974ft

An attractive, not over-strenuous climb with some boggy sections which gives good close views of Pen y Ghent and a panorama of Malham Tarn and Upper Airedale. The terrain alternates betwen gritstone and limestone.

Park on wide verge near entrance to Tennant Gill Farm. SD884691. To get there take M62/M6 to J31, A59 to Gisburn and A682/A65 to Settle. Drive under railway arch and turn right on B6479. At Langcliffe turn right on minor road signposted for Malham and after 6.4km/4ml turn left at signpost to Arncliffe. Park on left by farm entrance after second cattle-grid.

Walk up farm road and follow Pennine Way signpost on stony track passing farm on right. After gate, track turns left and then right at signpost. At large cairn fork right to contour hillside and follow clear track. Extensive boggy area by second stream can be turned by circuit to left. Wall crosses at highest point of track.

Turn left with wall on right to reach massive cairn on summit of fell. Turn SE to visit large tarn and then rejoin wall. Cross wall on minor summit (662m on map) where it is broken and continue S with wall on left.

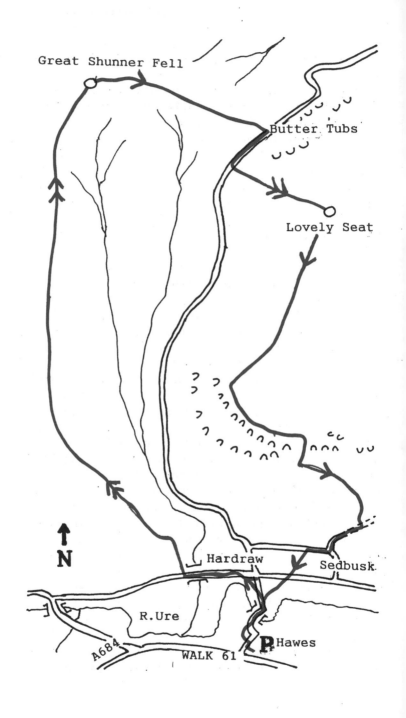

Great Shunner Fell

Butter Tubs

Lovely Seat

N

Hardraw

Sedbusk

R.Ure

A684

WALK 61

P Hawes

Turn right on meeting crossing wall and follow it S again when it turns. Continue for 2.4km/1.5ml to reach TP.

Go through gap in wall SE of TP and go E (no path), heading for large barn conspicuous on hillside opposite. Gradually an old wall, one or two stones high, is visible on left. Follow this down until it joins a proper wall at a corner. A dilapidatcd ladder stile will be found. Cross this and go NE on path, not always too clear. In first field leave track curving right to reach small gate ahead. Path then crosses another old ladder stile, a stone step stile and a gate in a wire fence. Go down to right to gate in corner of field on lane where car is parked.

It is not practicable to shorten this walk.

61. *Great Shunner Fell and Lovely Seat*

Ordnance Survey Map No: 98 or OL No 30
Distance from city centre: 171km/107ml
Walking distance: 22.5km/14ml
Amount of climbing: 621m/2050ft

A hard walk needing a long day out but offering contrasts between peat-hags and limestone terraces. Normally you are likely to meet only Pennine Way walkers.

Park in National Park Centre in Hawes. SD875899. To get there take the M62/M6 to J37 and the A684 to Hawes. Parking is off A684 on left at E end of town.

Follow the Pennine Way, which is well waymarked, to the summit of Great Shunner Fell. From the carpark cross the disused railway, turn right on the Hardraw road and then left over a stile at the first PW marker to follow the Way to Hardraw village (diversion through the Green Dragon Inn to see waterfall recommended – small fee) From pub door turn right, cross bridge and then right again to follow PW N along the ridge to Great Shunner Fell.

Leave the PW and go SE keeping always to the highest ground to drop down to the Buttertubs (limestone formations) on the Hawes/Thwaite road. Turn

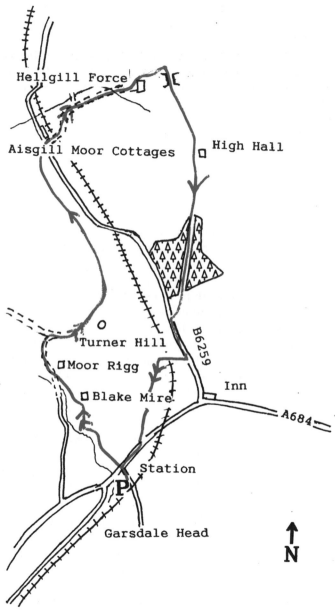

Hellgill Force

Aisgill Moor Cottages

High Hall

Turner Hill

Moor Rigg

Blake Mire

B6259

Inn

A684

Station

P

Garsdale Head

N

Walk 62

right to the top of the pass until you see a fence on left which leads from a cattle-grid directly SE to the summit of Lovely Seat.

From the summit go SSW with the road parallel on right until meeting a bridleway going SE. Follow the waymarks down to a walled lane leading to Sedbusk village. Turn right at the road, then left over a stile, and down to a lane. Go through gate on other side and follow footpath to road. Turn left back to Hawes.

This walk can be shortened by returning direct to Hawes from the Buttertubs. Save 4km/2.5ml.

62.   Garsdale Head

Ordnance Survey Map No: 98
Distance from city centre: 162km/101ml
Walking distance: 12.75km/8ml
Amount of climbing: 320/1060ft

Although the mileage to the start of this walk is high, the journey does not take long by the M6. The area is remote and less inhabited than it was 50 years ago and there are many desolate ruins to be seen. Paths are generally indistinct and the walk is best kept for clear weather. The route crosses the Settle-Carlisle Railway at Aisgill Summit, its highest point. You could consider travelling by train to experience the superb scenery en route.

Park at roadside near Garsdale Station. SD788918. To get there take M62/M6 to J37 and A684 (Hawes road). Turn right up lane to Garsdale Station 5km/3ml past Garsdale village. Park where convenient.

From station go down to main road, cross, go over stile opposite and walk NW with wall on left. Path drops to stream and then goes N over hill to Blake Mire. Signposts and stiles indicate route NW and then N to lane at Moor Rigg. Turn right on lane to East House.

Go past farm and through gate. Track turns sharply right and joins another track. Turn right and after 100m/110yd turn left NE uphill to pass through gate just NW of highest point, Turner Hill, on right of way but with no path to be seen. Follow wall on right until it turns right and then go N along valley parallel to road and railway on right. Route passes disused farm (High Shaw Paddock) and goes through series of gates with wall on right, down to road at Aisgill Moor Cottages.

Cross road and railway bridge and follow track past Hell Gill Force on left. Cross stream and go up past farm to Hell Gill Bridge. Turn right on old track, the High Way. After 190m/200yd on green track, go up left on path to gate in wall corner. Path stays at high level crossing streams and following walls on right.

Cross ford before ruins of High Hall 1.3km/0.8ml past Hell Gill Bridge and take track down to right through gates to pick up series of gates and stiles. Plantation across valley gives general direction S. Cross farm access road through gates and continue to footbridge and stile. Turn right, pass Lunds Chapel on left and cross river into plantation. When track curves right go left at footpath sign and follow path through plantation and over stiles down to road. Turn left.

After 0.4km/0.25ml take signposted footpath on right and cross railway. Go uphill looking for first of four stiles indicating route until reaching road with farm 200m/220yd on left. Turn right to lane up to railway station.

It is not practicable to shorten this walk.

Walk 70   Ashurst Beacon

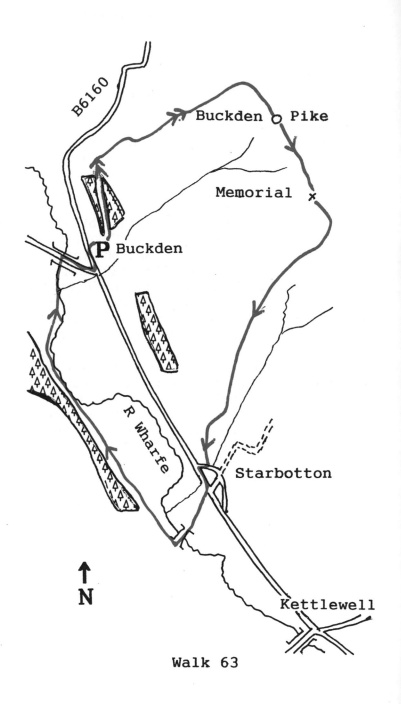

Walk 63

63. *Buckden Pike*

Ordnance Survey Map No: 98 or OL 30
Distance from city centre: 150km/94ml
Walking distance: 12km/7.5ml
Amount of climbing: 490m/1615ft

Buckden, like many parts of the Dales, has an extensive history. This walk begins on a Roman road and passes a memorial to the victims of a later conflict: five Polish airmen whose bomber crashed on the summit in the snows of January 1942.

Carpark at the N end of Buckden village. SD943774. To get there take the M62/M6 to J31. Take the A59 and turn left on to the B6265 on Skipton bypass. At Threshfield turn left on to the B6160 to Buckden.

From the back of the carpark a track leads N to the top of a wood. Turn up by the wall at the second gate and follow the path NE through gates on to the moor to a wall where a bridleway sign to Buckden Pike points SE to TP on the summit.

Cross wall at summit and continue alongside wall on right to the memorial cross. When wall turns right go through gate and descend to B6160 to Starbotton. Turn left and then right between walls on track leading to bridge. Cross R. Wharfe and turn right to follow riverside path (Dales Way) to bridge at Buckden. Turn right to village.

It is not practicable to shorten this walk.

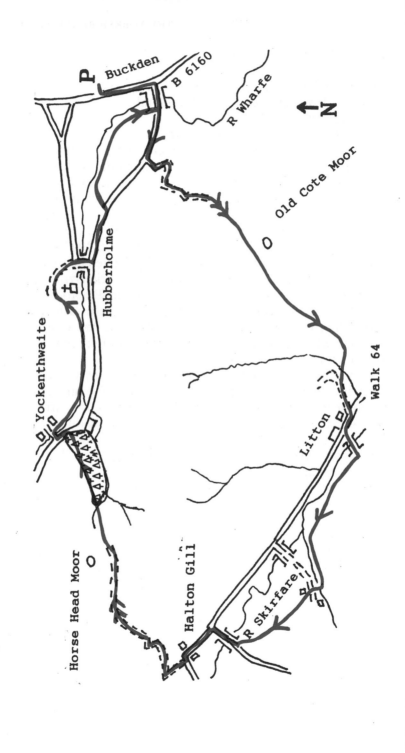

64. Old Cote Moor and Horse Head Moor

Ordnance Survey Map No: 98 or OL No 30
Distance from city centre: 150km/94ml
Walking distance: 20km/12.5ml
Amount of climbing: 690m/2280ft

The fell between the R. Skirfare the R. Wharfe provides some excellent walking; unfortunately there is no path or right of way along the ridge and in order to enjoy it, you have to perm any two of the five routes which cross from one side to the other. This makes for a relatively long day out for this area.

Carpark at the N end of Buckden village. SD943774. To get there take the M62/M6 to J31. Take the A59 and turn left on to the B6265 on the Skipton bypass. At Threshfield turn left on to the B6160 to Buckden.

From carpark go back to village and down to bridge over Wharfe. Cross and 350m/300yd up road turn left on to well signposted bridleway past Redmire Farm and up on to open moor, where route is indicated by stakes. On reaching wall on left go through gap and continue with wall on right. At cross wall TP is on left. Descend with wall on right, crossing it as route turns sharply right just above a wood and goes over a beck. As you come into Litton you will be glad to note the Queen's Head.

Make your way down to the bridge, cross, turn right and follow the riverside path. At Hesleden Beck the path detours left to cross it and then continues N and NE past a line of traditional Dales barns before coming back to river and Halton Gill Bridge.

Cross river and turn left into Halton Gill. Just after lane turns sharply left a lane with wall on left goes off to right. Go up this track and keep on it when it turns sharp right (footpath goes straight ahead to wall). Track winds upwards, going gradually right to wall which meets cross wall on summit.

Path now descends NE, passing wood on right, and joins road at Raisgill Farm. Turn left and cross next bridge on right into Yockenthwaite. Here turn right

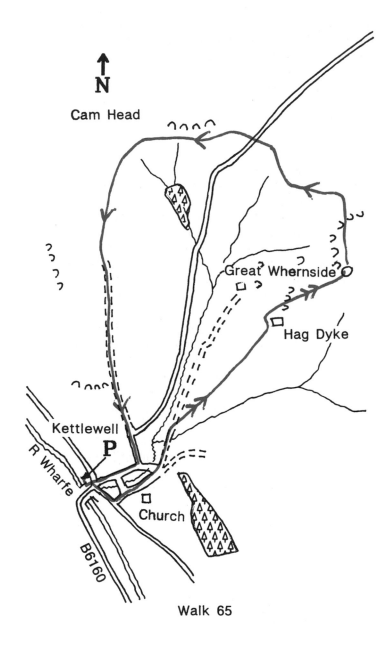

N

Cam Head

Great Whernside

Hag Dyke

Kettlewell

P

R Wharfe

B6160

Church

Walk 65

and follow Wharfe on Dales Way to Hubberholme. Cross river, turn left on road and after 650m/0.4ml take footpath on left (Dales Way) back to riverbank and to bridge in Buckden. Carpark is to left.

It is not possible to shorten this walk.

65. *Great Whernside*

Ordnance Survey Map No: 98 or OL No 30
Distance from city centre: 144km/90ml
Walking distance: 14km/8.5ml
Amount of climbing: 534m/1762ft

A steep climb up a most impressive face leading to a rocky summit leaves no doubt in the mind of the walker that this fell deserves its name. The views from the top can be quite outstanding.

Park in Kettlewell immediately on left after crossing R. Wharfe. SD968723. To get there take M62/M6 to J31 and A59 E. Turn left on to B6265 on Skipton bypass and at Threshfield turn left on to B6160 to Kettlewell.

From the carpark turn left and then fork right and left to pass church. Pass bridge where metalled road goes left and stay on a rough track with beck on left. Cross by next bridge and fork left up green lane signposted Hag Dyke (a Scouts' Outdoor Centre). Follow the lane to the Centre and go left of buildings to stile and cairns. Follow path NE through bog at first, direct to triangulation station on summit.

From summit go N for 1.6km/1ml until reaching the corner of a wall. Turn left to follow the wall W at first to road over Park Rash. Cross road and continue on grass track by wall contouring round hillside.

Shortly after the wall goes S the track forks at a signpost. Take left-hand fork S down the obvious ridge of Cam Head and continue when it becomes enclosed right down to Kettlewell. Turn right for carpark.

It is not practicable to shorten this walk except by turning SW on the Park Rash road, but the saving in distance is negligible.

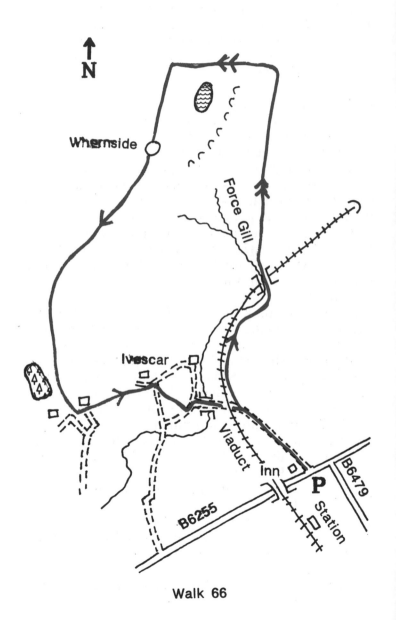

N

Whernside

Force Gill

Ivescar

Viaduct

Inn

P

B6479

Station

B6255

Walk 66

66. *Whernside*

Ordnance Survey Map No: 98 or OL No 2
Distance from city centre: 146km/91ml
Walking distance: 12.8km/8ml
Amount of climbing: 450m/1485ft

The highest of the "Yorkshire Three Peaks" and like the other two, subject to erosion through popularity, especially on the direct ascent from the E which this route avoids.

Park off B6255 near the Station Inn at Ribblehead just before junction with B6479. SD764791. To get there take M62/M6 to J34 and A683/A687/A65 to Ingleton. Turn on to B6255 to Hawes. Ribblehead is 11km/7ml NW. Parking on right.

Take stony track going NW towards the viaduct but leave it when it goes underneath and keep ahead parallel to viaduct, crossing railway line by the side of an aqueduct (detour uphill to view waterfall of Force Gill and return). Follow bridleway NW by fence and when this meets a wall follow wall W to ridge and then S to triangulation station on summit.

To descend, continue S to a cairn where path drops steeply to a walled lane. Turn left through gate to Ivescar Farm, turn right along farm road and then left over the first of a series of stiles leading to another farm road. Turn left, go over bridge on right and follow track back to car parking.

It is not practicable to shorten this walk.

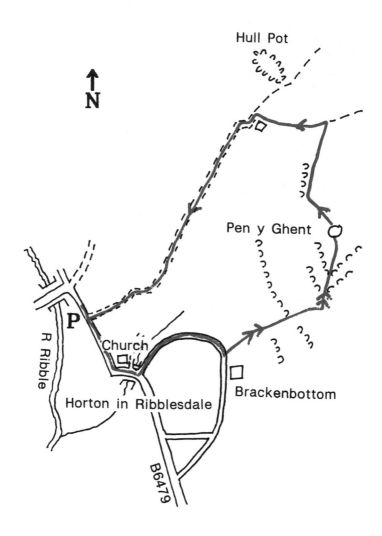

Hull Pot

N

Pen y Ghent

P

Church

Horton in Ribblesdale

Brackenbottom

R Ribble

B6479

Walk 67

67. *Pen y Ghent*

Ordnance Survey Map No: 98 or OL No 2
Distance from city centre: 138km/86ml
Walking distance: 9.5km/6ml
Amount of climbing: 464m/1540ft

Popular as one of the "Yorkshire Three Peaks", Pen y Ghent is also crossed by the Pennine Way. All walkers will want to tackle it, however, despite the erosion, which is now being seriously tackled.

Carpark in the centre of Horton in Ribblesdale. SD807726. To get there take M62/M6 to J31. Take A59, turn left at Gisburn on A682 and then left on A65. Drive into Settle and at the N end of the town turn right on B6479 to Horton. Carpark on left.

From the carpark turn right towards the church and just past it, over the bridge, turn left up a lane. Turn left at a signpost to Pen y Ghent just before Brackenbottom, over a stile and with a wall on left climb to the ridge which leads to the summit. Here turn left and climb steeply with wall on left all the way to the triangulation station on top.

To descend, cross the wall and go NNW on a stony track. On reaching a limestone cliff turn sharp left to the W (signpost Horton) and cross the moor by a made path to a walled lane. To see Hull Pot detour 300m/0.2ml right and return. Follow lane left down to Horton, taking right-hand fork near village.

It is not practicable to shorten this walk.

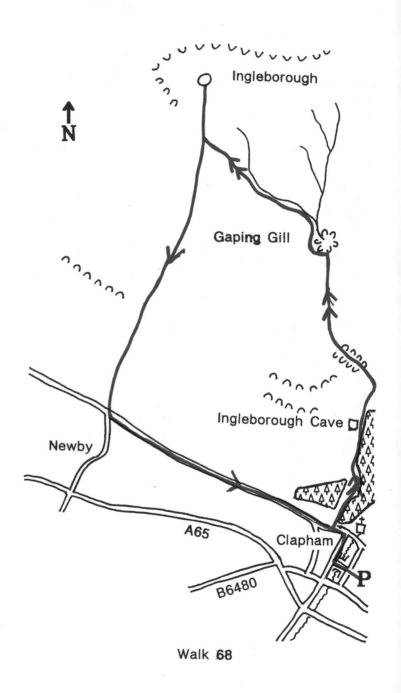

Ingleborough

Gaping Gill

Ingleborough Cave

Newby

A65

Clapham

P

B6480

Walk 68

68. *Ingleborough*

Ordnance Survey Map No: 98 or OL No 2
Distance from city centre: 141km/88ml
Walking distance: 12.75km/8ml
Amount of climbing: 550m/1815ft

One of the "Yorkshire Three Peaks" and a must for all walkers. Route-finding on the summit plateau can be difficult in bad weather.

Carpark in Clapham village. SD745692. To get there take M62/M6 to J34. Turn on to A683/A687/A65 to Ingleton and then to Clapham.

Turn right from the carpark, cross the footbridge and continue to N end of village, following lane as it turns left. After 100m/110yd take signposted track on right going N. Continue past woods, dropping down to stream and past Ingleborough Cave. Keep on this track which turns NW to emerge on the open moor. Follow a well trodden track NNW to view Gaping Gill and then keep left of stream until the path goes NW to a cairn on the edge of the plateau at Little Ingleborough. Go directly N for the triangulation station and wind shelter on the summit.

To descend, return to the cairn on Little Ingleborough but take the right of way going SW. The track is not clear and a compass bearing is advisable. Newby village comes into sight and the track makes straight towards it. On meeting a wall, follow it down to a stile by the lane and turn left for Clapham.

It is not practicable to shorten this walk.

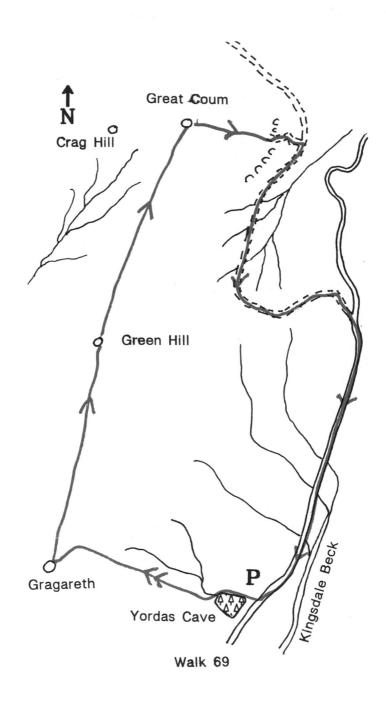

N

Crag Hill

Great Coum

Green Hill

Gragareth

Yordas Cave

P

Kingsdale Beck

Walk 69

69. Gragareth and Great Coum

Ordnance Survey Map No: 98 or OL No 2
Distance from city centre: 141km/88ml
Walking distance: 15km/9ml
Amount of climbing: 437m/1442ft

A fine, high-level walk with the option of a visit to an "unimproved" cave (good torch needed).

Park by the side of the road leading from Ingleton to Dent. SD706791. To get there take M62/M6 to J34 and A683/A687 to its junction with A65. Go down the lane directly opposite, and take the first left and the second right past Thornton in Lonsdale church. After 65km/4ml there is a small wood on left by Yordas cave and adequate off-road parking.

A gate gives access to the hillside and to Yordas cave on left. A path goes right, crosses the dry stream bed to the left and goes through a gate higher up. From here a wall can be followed to the ridge. The triangulation station on the summit is 0.4km/0.25ml SW.

Return E to the wall and follow it over Green Hill NNE, through a gate and to a cross wall on top of Great Coum. The summit cairn is on the far side of the wall.

The descent is by the wall running SE. When this is succeeded by a fence, cross and with the fence on left go down to a gate on the track below (Occupation Road). Here turn right and follow the track as it curves round to its junction with a lane. Turn right and follow this back for 3.6km/2.25ml to Yordas cave.

It is not practicable to shorten this walk.

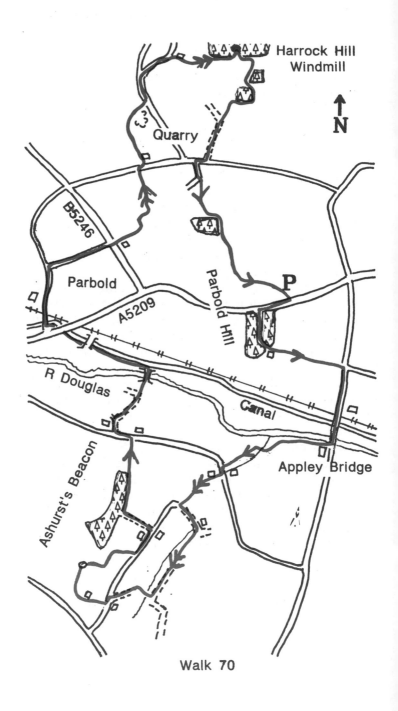

Harrock Hill
Windmill

N

Quarry

B5246

Parbold

Parbold Hill

P

A5209

R Douglas

Canal

Appley Bridge

Ashurst's Beacon

Walk 70

THE PENNINES

70. Parbold Hill

Ordnance Survey Map No: 108
Distance from city centre: 32km/20ml
Walking distance: 18km/11.25ml
Amount of climbing: 310m/1025ft

About the nearest hills to Liverpool and offering extensive views in clear weather. The route is often muddy and perhaps best left for a dry spell or when the ground is frozen. Very few footpaths are signposted.

Park in a large lay-by N side of A5209. SD516109. To get there take A59 and turn right on to A5209 just before Burscough Bridge. Parking is on left, 0.6km/ 0.4ml beyond the summit of Parbold Hill. As the walk passes both Parbold and Appley Bridge stations, it could be reached by rail.

From the lay-by turn right, cross the road at a foot-path sign and go down track opposite. At the end of the fence follow the track down to left and then turn right, following the stream on left. Cross at the second bridge and follow stream on right as far as a fence and stile (third bridge below on right). Cross stile and turn right on lane as far as farm gate. Go over stile on left across field to left of house, cross drive and continue to Skull House Lane. Turn right past railway station, over canal and over river. Turn immediately right and, on reaching an isolated stile, turn half-left towards hedge (waymarker) and follow it to the right to stream. Cross, turn left and follow path by stream to lane. Turn left and then right up lane by next house and when it turns left by farm take track on right through trees. Where track turns left drop down to stream on right, cross and follow track round hillside to lane. Turn left and at road left again and after a few yards turn right on path by holly trees. At stile go half-right to driveway and cross to path with pond on left. Turn right on track and up to Ashurst Beacon with views across to the sea W, to the N and to the Pennines E.

Take a bearing E from Beacon to join a track and follow it to the left, across a stile. Go round edge of field on right, cross stile and bridge and follow field edge down to lane. Turn left and left again on track opposite Bangham Farm. When this reaches wood, track goes right and down to road by left of fields. Turn left on road and then up driveway of next farm on right, forking right and following concrete drive. Where this curves left keep ahead to cross river and reach canal. Turn left on towpath to the bridge in Parbold (after sharp turn left). Go up to road, turn right, cross railway line and turn right past shops (Tan House Lane). At T-Junction cross road and keep ahead up lane opposite (school on right). Follow hedge on left and cross footbridge on left. Go half-left to pond with trees, up to stile and over field to metal gate on road. Turn right and then left over stile before house, keeping to right of field. Go over stile to stone wall and follow it to track. Turn right and then left at fork and go past houses and quarries to road.

Turn downhill and then right at Jackson's Lane. Take fork right going straight through gentrified farmyard and up concrete drive. When this turns right keep ahead with wire fence and then wall on right. Go through edge of wood and then up to see ruins of windmill on left. Return to wall, turn left and then right by next gate and keep fence on left around right-hand edge of plantation and up to left-hand edge of next plantation. Turn right at top of trees and follow clear path down to driveway. Turn left, then right at road. Cross and go left down lane, keeping straight ahead when it turns right. At end of hedge on left turn half-left by telegraph pole to middle of plantation ahead. Turn left and follow path round end of plantation. Go downhill with stream on left, through trees. Cross stream at end of wood, over stile and follow left-hand edge of field to stile in lay-by.

This walk could be done as two separate loops using the Leeds–Liverpool canal from Parbold to Appley Bridge and starting at one of those villages. The N loop would be 13km/8ml and the S, 12km/7.5ml, with 150m/500ft of climbing in each.

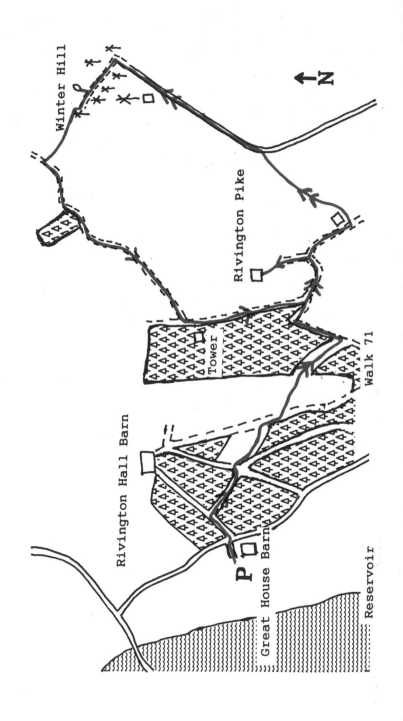

N

Winter Hill

Rivington Pike

Rivington Hall Barn

Tower

Walk 71

Great House Barn

P

Reservoir

71.   Rivington Pike and Winter Hill

Ordnance Survey Map No: 109
Distance from city centre: 69km/43ml
Walking distance: 12.5km/7.8ml
Amount of climbing: 376m/1240ft

A good introduction to the West Pennine Moors, with stretches of parkland laid out by Lord Lever-hulme, woodlands, moorlands and some modern technology.

Park at the Great Barn carpark and Information Centre, Rivington. SD628138. To get there take the M62/M6 to J27, A5209 to Standish, B5239 to Aspull and B5238 to Horwich. At T-junction in Horwich turn left and almost immediately right, signposted West Pennine Moors. Carpark is 2km/1.25ml on left. Further ample parking signposted nearby.

From carpark return to road, cross and go along access road signposted to Rivington Hall. Take first gravelled track on right and where this meets another large track take a small footpath straight ahead. Cross a meadow keeping to the right until meeting another gravelled track. Turn right, cross a low stile and turn uphill to left on a stony track.

On meeting another track, turn left and continue uphill as the track zigzags to meet yet another track. Turn right for 200m/220yd and go through a gate on left to gain access to Rivington Pike. Return to this point and continue SE to an isolated house on left. Immediately beyond it a stile on left leads to an easily followed track over the moor, which joins the access road to the radio transmitters on Winter Hill. Turn left on this road and go past the main transmitter and the associated buildings on left and looking out for the Scotsman's Stump on right. Follow the road as it bends left to pass between some smaller transmitters. The TP is right of the route. At the end of the road a transmitter is directly in front. Pass right of this and a footpath, small at first but becoming more obvious, leads downhill to a bridge and a stony track.

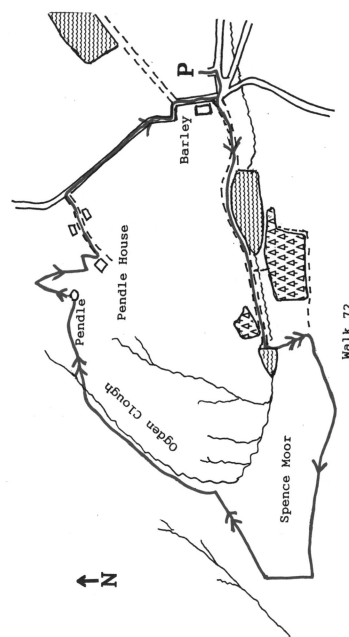

Turn left and stay on this track until reaching a tower at the top of Lever Park. If you stay on this track you will reach the point at which you joined it on the outward leg. Turn right and reverse your outward route. If you wish to be more adventurous, go through the gate by the tower and explore the myriad paths leading downhill. By tending right you will reach either Rivington Hall or the road leading to it.

It is not practicable to shorten this walk.

72. *Pendle Hill*

Ordnance Survey Map No: 103
Distance from city centre: 110km/69ml
Walking distance: 10km/6ml
Amount of climbing: 337m/1112ft

One of Lancashire's most famous hills, dominating the landscape for many miles around. It has strong historical associations with the ill-fated Pendle witches.

Park at the Information Centre and picnic sites at Barley. SD882404. To get there take the M62/M6 to J31 and A59 (Clitheroe), turning left to Chatburn. In the village fork right to Downham. Fork right past church and turn right at next crossroads. Parking is on left.

From carpark cross road to village hall and take bridleway W to foot of dam at second reservoir. Cross dam and continue uphill. At top of ridge follow way-markers SW and then NW on to Spence Moor. Route is then marked N and NE leading into Ogden Clough.

Follow the clough and then the stream to cairn near source. A track then leads NE to TP on summit.

From summit go N to wall where track doubles back SE to join wall after 500m/550yd. It then goes left of Pendle House to join farm track. Turn left to reach lane and go right for 1.5km/0.8ml to car park.

It is not practicable to shorten this walk.

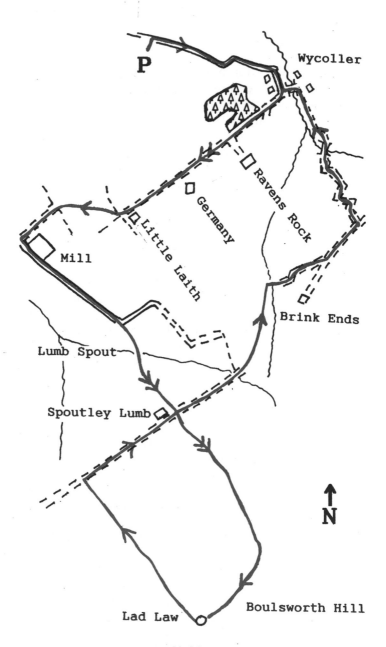

P

Wycoller

Ravens Rock

Germany

Little Laith

Mill

Lumb Spout

Brink Ends

Spoutley Lumb

N

Lad Law

Boulsworth Hill

Walk 73

73. *Boulsworth Hill*

Ordnance Survey Map No: 103 or OL No 21
Distance from city centre: 114km/71ml
Walking distance: 13.6km/8.5ml
Amount of climbing: 307m/1013ft

Access to this summit is by agreement with the NW Water Authority, but most of the walk is over farmland or in Wycoller Country Park. Much of the area between here and Haworth, including Wycoller Hall (now in ruins) has associations with the Brontë sisters. A centre of hand-loom weaving, Wycoller was deserted for over 150 years.

Park at Wycoller Country Park. SD926394. To get there take the M62/M6 to J31, A59/A677/A6119 (Blackburn bypass) and M65 to end. Turn left on to A56 and left again on to B6247 which skirts Colne town centre, in direction of Keighley. Turn left on to A6068 and after 2.5km/1.5ml turn right at Laneshaw-bridge (Country Park signposted – Haworth road). After 50m/55yd turn right again, following signs to Wycoller.

From carpark take lane E into Wycoller village. Past last houses take access road on right to Raven's Rock Farm. Steps on right go up to path and through plantation. Keep on path, passing Germany Farm on left. At Little Laith go due W downhill with wall on left to cross Trawden Brook and pass mill on left. Turn left at lane and where this turns sharp left keep straight on to pass through Lodge Moss Farm. Continue on path and cross stream. To view Lumb Spout waterfall turn right and then return and go uphill with wall on right to track by Spoutley Lumb Farm.

Go SE uphill on access strip to ridge and turn right (SW) to summit – Lad Law. Descent NW leads back to track. Turn right, pass Spoutley Lumb Farm again and continue on track with wall left.

At end of wall track changes to path which follows stream N for 500m/550yd, crosses it and continues on track going E. You are now on route of waymarked

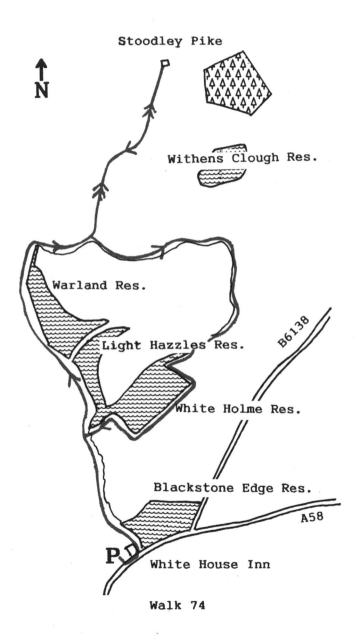

Stoodley Pike

N

Withens Clough Res.

Warland Res.

Light Hazzles Res.

B6138

White Holme Res.

Blackstone Edge Res.

A58

P

White House Inn

Walk 74

Pendle Way. Track rises to join access road to Brink Ends Farm and after 100m/110yd track from Wycoller joins from left. Turn left back to carpark.

This walk may be shortened by continuing left on lane instead of going to Lumb Spout. This comes out on lane beyond Spoutley Lumb Farm. Turn left to pick up Pendle Way. Save 4km/2.5ml.

74. Stoodley Pike

Ordnance Survey Map No: 109 and 103 or OL No 21
Distance from city centre: 72km/45ml
Walking distance: 19km/11.8ml
Amount of climbing: 65m/215ft

Stoodley Pike was built in celebration of the Peace of Ghent at which Napoleon abdicated. For the Pennine Way walker it is a landmark for so many days that as Barry Pilton remarks in his account of the walk, *One Man and his Bog*, it seems to be on wheels! This walk follows the Way to the monument and returns on a permitted path by water-gathering drains and a reservoir. There is very little climbing.

Park below the White House Inn on the A58. SD968178. To get there take M62 to J21 and A663 to Milnrow. After 1km/0.5ml turn right on B6225 to Littleborough and right on A58. Parking is on the left before inn.

From carpark turn up left past inn and take Water Company's gravelled road on left with reservoir on right. Keep alongside two more reservoirs. At end of second, track follows concrete drain, first NNE, then ESE and finally NE. When drain turns SE (followed from here on return) cairns lead N on Pennine Way and then NNE. Keep to the left-hand edge of escarpment and head for monument.

Return to drain and follow it SE and then as it contours E, S and SW to White Holme Reservoir. Turn left to follow S bank back to Pennine Way by Light Hazzles Reservoir. Turn left and retrace outward route.

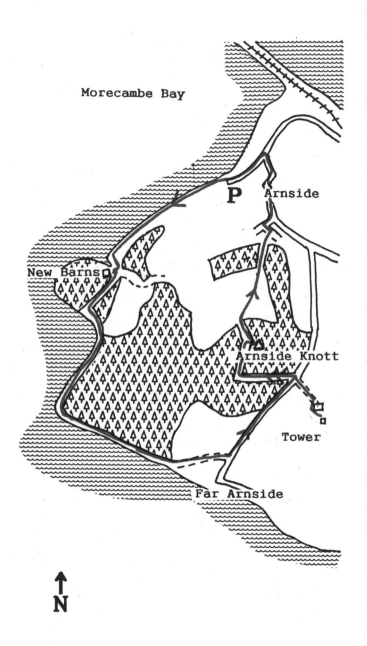

Morecambe Bay

P Arnside

New Barns

Arnside Knott

Tower

Far Arnside

N

Walk 75

It is possible to shorten this walk by turning SE on the drain and omitting the section to Stoodley Pike. Save 4.8km/3ml.

75. *Arnside Knott*

Ordnance Survey Map No: 97
Distance from city centre: 133km/83ml
Walking distance: 10.4km/6.5ml
Amount of climbing: 159m/525ft

A fine limestone hill and an Area of Outstanding Natural Beauty, Arnside Knott is worth visiting, especially in autumn and winter, just for the bird life on the estuary. It is also rich in caravan sites and you can visit a 14th-century pele tower built as a defence against border raiders.

Park on the promenade in Arnside. SD454786. To get there take M62/M6 to J35, A6 to Milnthorpe and B5282 to Arnside.

From parking area walk to end of promenade and continue SW on foot path by beach, crossing bay and taking track on left through woods after passing New Barns on right on far side. On reaching shore again, turn left to follow shoreline over low cliffs to Far Arnside. Path goes through caravan site and along lane to T-junction. Turn left and then turn right along farm track to visit tower and return.

Cross road entering National Trust property and go left uphill on track. After 0.8km/0.5ml take path on right. Turn right at T-junction to reach summit.

To descend, go NNW for 250m/275yd, across stile and descend grassy slope to stile into woods half-right. At road turn left, then right at T-junction and follow road down to promenade.

It is possible to shorten this walk by omitting the visit to the tower. Save 0.6km/0.4ml.

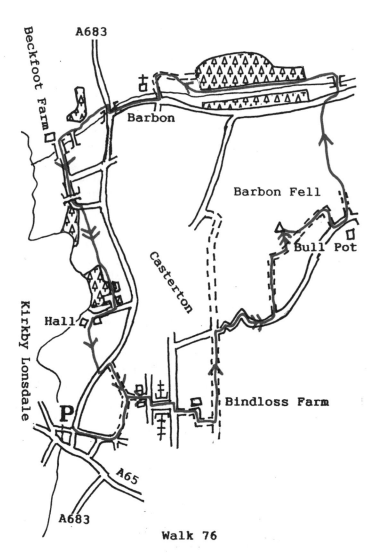

N

A683

Beckfoot Farm

Barbon

Barbon Fell

Kirkby Lonsdale

Casterton

Bull Pot

Hall

Bindloss Farm

P

A65

A683

Walk 76

76. Barbon Fell

Ordnance Survey Map No: 97 and 98
Distance from city centre: 131km/82ml
Walking distance: 18.4km/11.5ml
Amount of climbing: 455m/1501ft

A mixture of quiet lanes, bridleways and paths; pastoral lowland and open moorland; woods and riverside paths. With so many other attractions nearby, this area tends to be undervalued by walkers.

Park near the Devil's Bridge, Kirkby Lonsdale. SD616782. To get there take M62/M6 to J34 and A683 to Kirkby Lonsdale. At junction with A65 turn left and then right on A683 (Sedbergh). Small carpark on left; larger carpark on right.

Go up small lane in left corner of large carpark. Turn left on track at signpost for Colliers Lane and at junction of tracks turn right at signpost. Continue between houses and turn right at lane. Pass under railway bridge and turn right at junction. Turn left at signpost for Fell Road. Pass Bindloss Farm on left, turn right with wall on left, go through gate and turn left on track between walls. At gate turn left on track leading to lane. Turn right.

Lane climbs steeply. After 700m/0.4ml turn left on stony track. Past gate turn right on to open moor. Through next gate go up to TP on summit and return to track. At fork go right and rejoin lane. Turn left. Where road turns sharp right by Bull Pot Farm turn sharp left on track. Maintain direction on fainter paths beyond gate to reach lane in Barbondale. Turn right, cross bridge and turn left, following path through woods with stream on left into grounds of Barbon Manor. Go down estate road, cross bridge and turn right by church into village and down to A683.

Turn right, cross bridge and go over road to gate and path through new golf course. Pass through gateway half right by wall and power line. Continue with hedge and then wood on right and at corner of wood keep ahead to river bank and cross stile. Follow power lines to river and walk on riverside to Beckfoot Farm. Cross river, noting ancient bridge on left. Lane passes under estate bridge.

At the end of wood right go through second of pair of new gates to climb with wall on right. Go through gate with wall now on left. At bend maintain direction to ladder stile and then stile by wood. Follow edge of wood and enter by kissing gate in corner. Maintain direction through wood, across meadow and next wood. Turn right at junction and go right on bend at waymark. Follow waymarks through kissing gate and follow edge of field.

Right of way passes through grounds of hall. Maintain direction through gate, across courtyard, under arch and through door with waymark. Continue under arch and cross drive to kissing gate. Path between wire fences leads to A683. Cross road, turn left and after 150m/165yd turn right on waymarked track by Casterton golf course. At junction of tracks turn right and retrace footsteps to carpark.

To shorten this walk do not turn right up the lane reached after Bindloss Farm. Cross lane and follow track down to next lane. Turn right and follow enclosed lane to next junction. Turn left to join main route by Barbon Church. Save 5.6km/3.5ml.

Walk 70   Ruined windmill on Harrock Hill

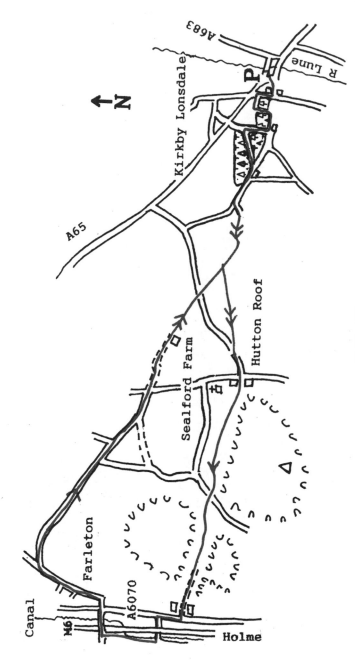

N

A683

R Lune

Kirkby Lonsdale

P

A65

Hutton Roof

Sealford Farm

Farleton

Canal

M6

A6070

Holme

Walk 77

77. Hutton Roof

Ordnance Survey Map No: 97
Distance from city centre: 134km/84ml
Walking distance: 21km/13ml
Amount of climbing: 330m/1090ft

Recent local initiatives to encourage walking in this area have resulted in the establishment of The Limestone Link from Kirkby Lonsdale to Arnside. This walk makes use of its eccentric blue waymarking (standard for bridleways) as far as the canal at Holme. It returns by footpaths and some of the narrowest and quietest lanes I have met anywhere.

Park on W side of the Devil's Bridge off A65 outside Kirkby Lonsdale. SD614783. To get there take M62/M6 to J36 and A65 to Kirkby Lonsdale. Parking is on left 100m/110yd beyond B6254 crossroads into town.

Go down steps by bridge on to river bank on W side and take path half-right across field to stile on road. *Crossing here can be dangerous.* On far side of road go through stile and over field, passing between houses. Turn right on lane and go over stile into field, keeping to left-hand edge by wood on left. Go through wood at gate, continuing uphill with wood now on right. Pass through farmyard on to lane and turn right. After 100m/110yd take footpath signposted left through small wood and at lane turn right. After 400m/0.25ml turn left on track. Limestone Link is now signposted.

Go right through squeeze stile and over brow of hill, following track half-left and half-right. When directly above barn, below to left, turn downhill by post carrying telephone cables, go through gate and follow signposts W over brow of hill to lane at Hutton Roof.

Turn left on lane, and at T-junction cross lane and go up steep path directly opposite, between houses. This path contours slopes of Hutton Roof Crags. The summit is 1.6km/0.6ml S and can be visited, but the area is a complex of paths and deserves a day of exploration to itself.

At next lane take path almost opposite and continue

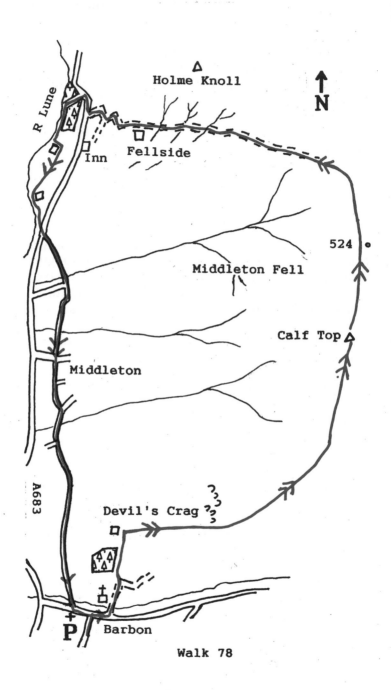

Holme Knoll

R Lune

Inn

Fellside

N

Middleton Fell

524

Calf Top

Middleton

A683

Devil's Crag

Barbon

P

Walk 78

W. Path becomes track with crags on both sides and drops down to A6070. Turn right.

Take lane left under M6, cross canal and turn right on towpath. Limestone Link goes left on towpath into Holme village, the only opportunity for refreshments on this walk.

When canal reaches M6 keep ahead parallel to motorway, turning right at lane to cross both and reach A6070 again. Cross into Farleton village and, ignoring three turnings to left, follow lane around fell until you are going SE. Pass lane from right and from left and at T-junction go straight ahead downhill on access road to Sealford Farm.

Cross stream and go uphill under power lines on track and then path to lane. Cross and keep going SE. After 0.8km/0.5ml outward route is joined above barn, below on right. Retrace outward route to carpark.

This walk can be shortened by turning right at T-junction at Hutton Roof. Pass church and lane on left and access road to Sealford is 1km/0.5ml beyond. Save 11km/7ml.

78. Middleton Fell and Calf Top

Ordnance Survey Map Nos: 97 and 98
Distance from city centre: 136km/85ml
Walking distance: 20km/12.5ml
Amount of climbing: 600m/1980ft

Do not be deterred by the road walk at the end of this route – the lane is extremely quiet and it is well worth it for the exhilarating, high-level sections. The area attracts few walkers as it lies between National Parks. Higher parts are difficult in mist.

Park (considerately) by village hall in Barbon. SD628824. To get there take M62/M6 to J34 and A683 (Kirkby Lonsdale). Turn left on A65 and right again to continue on A683 (Sedbergh). Turn right at sign for Barbon after 5km/3ml just before crossing R. Lune. Turn right at Cross in village. Carpark is 100m/110yd on right.

Return to Cross and turn right. Turn left over bridge by church on to metalled drive to Barbon Manor. Where drive straightens after bend go left and make for corner of wood NE. Continue with wood on left, pass through gate and turn up right by farm along line of trees to gate. Cross and go up steeply to right of Devil's Crag ahead and then to tall cairn on skyline.

Small but clear path now keeps to centre of broad ridge E and then NE over Castle Knott before dropping to col and rising to TP on Calf Top. Continue NE curving NW with wall on right for 4km/2.5ml to gate in wall on right and small stone shelter on left. Route (now vehicle track) swings away left from wall and leads down to Fellside Farm and A683. Turn right and cross road.

On left just past first bend go through gate on left on to bridleway through wood. By next gate right of way on left is obstructed – go through gate and on to river bank. Rejoin bridleway on far side of barn on left. Continue S with fence on left through gates to reach river bank again. Go through gates into farmyard and turn right between buildings. Go through gate and next gate on right. Walk close to fence on left with river on right and cross fence, gate and right gate of pair. Go around field edge on left to gate on to A683.

Turn right, cross and go down small lane on left. Ignore all turnings off and this leads directly to Barbon (5km/3ml) Turn left at junction and right at Cross to carpark.

Because there are few rights of way it is not possible to shorten this walk.

Walk 57   Cowper's Cross

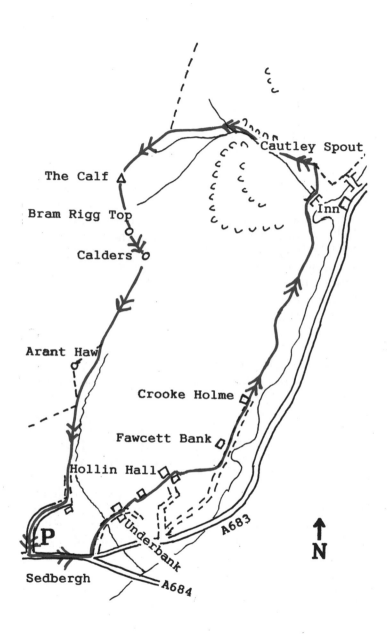

The Calf △

Bram Rigg Top ○

Calders ○

Arant Haw ○

Crooke Holme ▢

Fawcett Bank ▢

Hollin Hall ▢

Cautley Spout

Inn

P

Underbank

Sedbergh

A683

A684

N

Walk 79

79. Howgills – The Calf

Ordnance Survey Map Nos: 97 and 98
Distance from city centre: 147km/92ml
Walking distance: 16km/10ml
Amount of climbing: 624m/2059ft

The Howgill Fells consist of a huge area of land with few walls or features. Walks are generally long and the best routes are linear. This walk leaves Sedbergh by paths and bridleways and ascends by Cautley Spout, the best known feature in the area. The return is a high-level traverse, which can be difficult in mist.

Park in Sedbergh near the Information Office. SD599922. To get there take M62/M6 to J37 and A684 to Sedbergh. Carpark at end of cobbled street on left. Another carpark near church.

Return to main road, turn left and after 250m/275yd turn left up steps in stone wall by signpost for Thorns Lane. Pass backs of houses and turn left on stony track. Pass between houses and through gate at Underbank and then through gate on left at footpath sign. Cross bridge and follow wall on right to stile in corner on to lane. Turn left and take right-hand fork. Cross cattle-grid and follow waymark to right of barn. Cross bridge and field to gates through Hollin Hall farmyard. Go half-right to hedge and stile in corner. Head for left end of stone wall and then down right by waymarked stiles leading to lane. Turn left.

This lane becomes a track and then a path and leads to a plank bridge over stream from Cautley Spout 4km/2.5ml away. Cross, turn left and join a large track leading to foot of waterfall. Climb very steeply on a small track with the cascades left and do not cross stream on track above falls. Turn left on reaching broad track going S and then SW to summit of The Calf. Go SSE to col and then S to Bram Rigg Top. Continue S to wire fence, turn right and follow fence on left on track round corner, leaving it at the next corner. Track now goes SW. Diversion may be made by forking right over summit of Arant Haw and rejoining track.

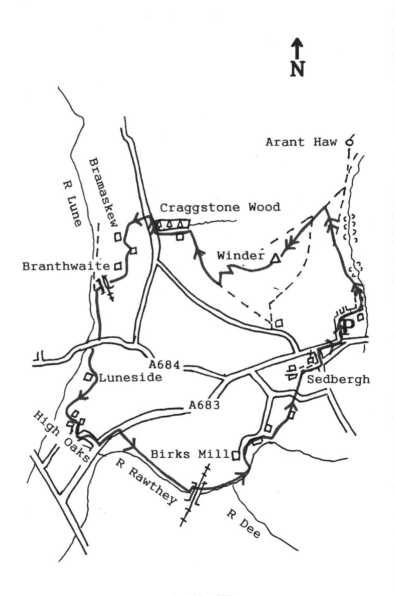

N

Arant Haw

Craggstone Wood

Bramaskew

R Lune

Winder

Branthwaite

A684

Luneside

A683

High Oaks

Birks Mill

Sedbergh

R Rawthey

R Dee

Walk 80

At cairn, fork left on track with stream and then ravine on left down to kissing gate by seat. Through gate, path leads to track and road through houses on to Joss Lane and carpark on left.

It is not practicable to shorten this walk except by hiring a taxi from Sedbergh to the Cross Keys Hotel on A683. Cross bridge W of hotel, turn left and follow track to waterfall to join main route. Save 6.4km/4ml.

Note: recommended additional map is Sedbergh (Howgills) by Stile Maps, available at Information Office, Sedbergh.

80. Howgills – Winder

Ordnance Survey Map No: 97
Distance from city centre: 147km/92ml
Walking distance: 14.4km/9ml
Amount of climbing: 393m/1297ft

This walk combines the classic ascent of Winder, the fell overlooking Sedbergh, with a return along river banks, part of the Dales Way.

Park in Sedbergh by the Information Office. SD649922. To get there take M62/M6 to J37 and A684 to Sedbergh. Carpark on left at end of cobbled street. Another carpark near church.

From carpark turn right up Joss Lane and follow signs "To the Fell" leading to stony track and way-marked path to kissing gate. Continue N keeping on track close to stream and ravine on right but at obvious fork go left to join broad green track by cairn. Turn left and follow track to summit of Winder.

Descend on broad track W down ridge and at wall turn right to gate by Craggstone Wood. Go through gate and follow stream. Do not go right to bridge but keep by wall and follow waymarks over stiles down to lane. Turn right. Near top of rise go through gate on left at signpost for Low Branthwaite. Keep hedge on left, pass farm on right, go through right-hand of pair of gates and cross farm road to gate marked "Dales Way". Path curves right by short section of wall to

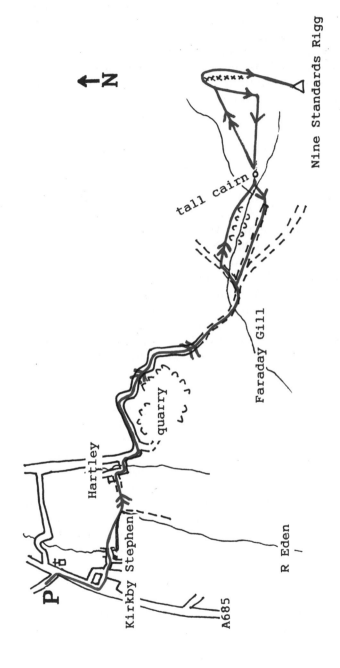

N

Nine Standards Rigg

tall cairn

Faraday Gill

quarry

Hartley

Kirkby Stephen

R Eden

A685

P

Walk 81

ladder stile and track. Turn left, cross bridge and immediately stile on right. Follow signpost for Lincoln's Inn Bridge.

Pass under old railway bridge and follow waymarks down to riverside path. Turn left. Cross road and turn right to stile to continue on river bank. After next stile leave river and go up left to stile. Follow fence on right to farm gate and go between buildings to track between hedges. Pass through gate by stone walls and maintain direction to hedge. Follow signpost for High Oaks and waymarks through restored buildings to lane. Turn left to reach A683.

After 1km/0.6ml turn right at signpost for Birks Mill to riverside path. At old railway bridge go left after crossing stile to find stepped path across tracks. Pass mill and continue on access road. Take footpath on right past cottages and curve left round back of house towards stone barn. Continue on track to lane. Cross and go through kissing gate opposite on path through school grounds. At junction turn right, pass church on left and reach lane. Turn left and then right for carpark.

To shorten this walk turn left instead of right at wall below Winder. This leads to access point by Lockbank Farm 0.8km/0.5ml away. Follow lane down, turning left for carpark. Save 8km/5ml.

81. Nine Standards Rigg

Ordnance Survey Map No: 91
Distance from city centre: 171km/107ml
Walking distance: 14.4km/9ml
Amount of climbing: 502m/1657ft

The purpose and origins of the group of cairns on this summit has long been the subject of speculation. For example, one theory holds that they were intended to appear like a group of armed men to deter Scottish border raiders. There is documentary evidence that they existed 200 years ago.

Park in Kirkby Stephen. NY773088. To get there take M62/M6 to J38 and A685 to Kirkby Stephen. At

N end of town fork left at Silver St. Carpark on left. Parking in Market Square and High Street is restricted in summer.

Return to Market Square and follow signposts to Frank's Bridge. Cross and turn right on riverbank. Go through gate and uphill on surfaced footpath leading to lane. Turn right, cross bridge and turn right on lane. Follow lane to its end at gate on to open fell.

Continue on stony track and cross stream. When wall bends right note tall cairn in nick above stream, Faraday Gill – this is next objective. Take left-hand fork down to stream and cross. When ground levels, fork right (no path) towards stream and climb with stream and then small gorge on right. Cross stream by sheepfold on left and then climb to cairn.

Cross little track beyond the tall cairn on faint path going E towards left-hand side of Nine Standards on skyline. Just below ridge note small cairn on crossing path. From summit cairns go S for panorama table and TP.

Walk 81   The Nine Standards

Walk 30   On Offa's Dyke

Return to summit cairns and descend to small cairn noted on path below. Path traverses hillside S before turning W straight onwards towards tall cairn passed on ascent. Turn left on little track and at once right on grassy track with Faraday Gill again on right. This leads to track by wall. Turn right to join outward route.

To shorten this walk do not park in Kirkby Stephen but turn right beyond Silver Street at signpost to Hartley. Turn right at junction and drive to end of fell road where there are several parking spaces. Save 7.2km/4.5ml.

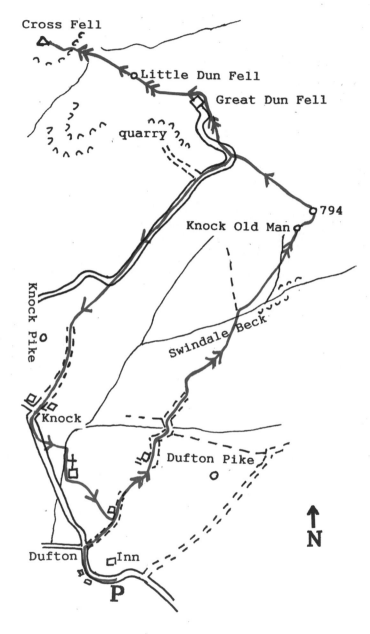

Cross Fell

Little Dun Fell

Great Dun Fell

quarry

794

Knock Old Man

Knock Pike

Swindale Beck

Knock

Dufton Pike

Dufton

Inn

P

N

Walk 82

82. *Cross Fell*

Ordnance Survey Map No: 91
Distance from city centre: 179km/112ml
Walking distance: 25.6km/16ml
Amount of climbing: 1055m/3481ft

Among the most demanding walks in the book, this requires fitness and a long, fine day. Cross Fell is the highest point in the Pennines and subject to poor weather – do not attempt in mist as there is little waymarking on higher ground.

Park in Dufton. NY689250. To get there take M62/M6 to J38 and B6260 to Appleby. Cross river in town and turn left. Past town centre road goes under railway on right and is signposted to Dufton. Carpark on left.

From carpark turn left and walk through village. Turn right at Pennine Way signpost and pass through farmyard. Route is on track then follows PW waymarkers in field. Go through gate to rejoin track to and past farm. Beyond gate on left cross stream by ancient clapper bridge and keep on track between walls. Stay on grassy track at end of walls and turn left on to path by PW signpost. Cross two walls and a bridge and fork right by notice-board.

Past large cairn on skyline path becomes more distinct with occasional cairn or post. Cross stream. After steep rise to marker post path curves left to huge square cairn (Knock Old Man) and then goes NE to cairn at 794m on map. Path turns left, going N and then NNW. Follow line of metal posts joining route from left down to metalled access road to radar station on Great Dun Fell. Turn right and leave road at PW sign right. Go to right of radar station. Continue NNW to Little Dun Fell and Cross Fell. Ground in cols is very boggy.

Simplest route back is to retrace steps. Note that bearing from Cross Fell is initially E to the tall cairn.

An alternative, no shorter but usefully losing height quickly in bad weather, is to follow the access road past the two PW signs and for a further 2.4km/1.5ml until the road makes a sharp turn right. Leave road and continue SW on right of way (no path) aiming for summit of Knock Pike. This leads directly to partly filled in but still usable step stile in wall. Cross and continue in same direction until gate is visible to right in next wall. Past this an easily followed track leads down to Knock. In pasture do not go to gates on left but maintain direction to track between wall and hedge. Go through farmyard to road and turn left.

Go left at footpath sign to Dufton, cross stream and turn right. Follow waymarked path through churchyard and then line of trees SE. Cross stream and turn right for Dufton on joining PW.

This walk could be shortened by retracing steps from the cairn on Knock Old Man. This would save 11.25km/ 7ml and still be a good day out.

*Walk 83 and 84   Crinkle Crags (left), Bow Fell
and Angdale Pikes*

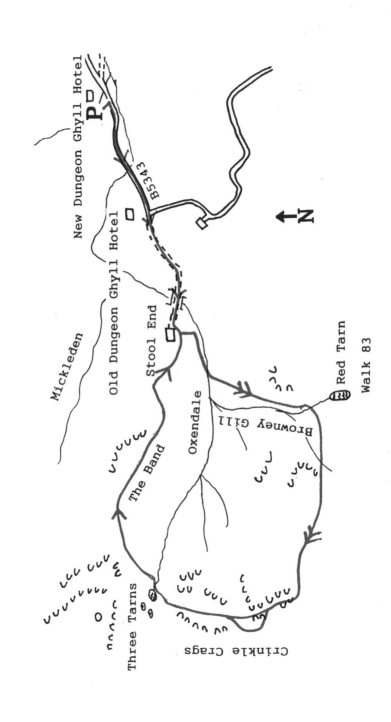

Walk 83

THE LAKE DISTRICT

83. Crinkle Crags

Ordnance Survey Map No: 90 or OL No 6
Distance from city centre: 168km/105ml
Walking distance: 13.5km/8.5ml
Amount of climbing: 788m/2600ft

A Lake District classic which will take longer than the mileage suggests as the terrain on the tops is rocky and entails a lot of scrambling up and down. The Crinkles ridge is very confusing and while this does not matter in good weather, it has caused difficulties in winter or in mist for more than one party. Save it to enjoy on a good day and go very early.

Park by the New Dungeon Ghyll Hotel. NY294063. To get there take M62/M6 to J36, A590/A591 to Windermere and Ambleside and A593 (Coniston). At Spark Bridge take B5343 into Langdale. Carpark is on right, 3.2km/2ml beyond Chapel Stile. Alternative carpark on left.

From carpark turn right on road and when it turns sharp left near Old Hotel keep straight ahead on access road to Stool End Farm. Keep left of farm to enter Oxendale on left. When path divides go left to cross stream by footbridge. Path up very steep hillside in front has been remade with many stone steps. It follows line of stream on right.

Before reaching Red Tarn, take track on right, cross-

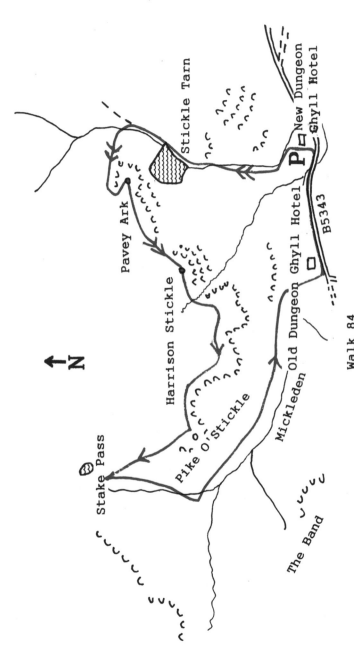

ing stream and going W. Follow cairns over gently rising plateau for 1.6km/1ml, gradually going NW, before first Crinkle is reached. Turn right. Route is worn and cairned and can be seen in clear weather. Drop into depression and go up gully ahead, using holds on right-hand wall. This is known as The Bad Step and can be avoided by going up easier rocks on left edge of gully or by making detour over easier ground left. General direction of Crinkles is N but path twists in and out with many alternatives and you need your wits about you to keep to highest ground. Views down rock gullies and buttresses to right are stupendous.

Route reaches col with three tarns, beyond which Bowfell rises up. Descend by The Band, the broad, grassy ridge on right. Go NE and cross stream. Track contours for 400m/440yd and then curves E before joining broad track which leads down to Stool End. Retrace outward route.

It is dangerous to try to shorten this route.

84. *The Langdale Pikes*

Ordnance Survey Map No: 90 or OL No 6
Distance from city centre: 168km/105ml
Walking distance: 13km/8ml
Amount of climbing: 740m/2450ft

The craggy profile of the Langdale Pikes is among the most photographed and most familiar of Lakeland scenes. There are attractions for the casual walker, the devoted fell walker, the scrambler and the rock climber within a very short distance of the valley carparks – and the pubs are good. Come early! Route finding needs care because of crags and this is not a route for bad weather.

Park by the New Dungeon Ghyll Hotel. NY294063. To get there take M62/M6 to J36, A590/A591 to Windermere and Ambleside and A593 (Coniston). At Spark Bridge take B5343 into Langdale. Carpark is on right,

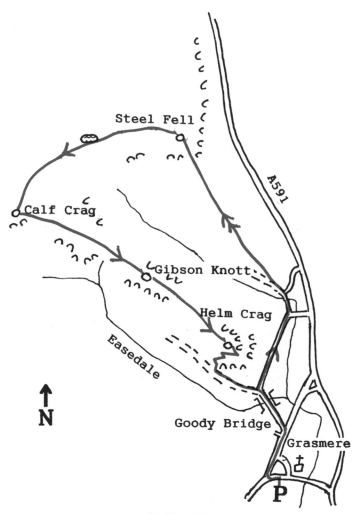

Steel Fell

A591

Calf Crag

Gibson Knott

Helm Crag

Easedale

Goody Bridge

Grasmere

P

N

Walk 85

3.2km/2ml beyond Chapel Stile. Alternative carpark on left.

At rear of carpark (N) gate with signpost for Stickle Ghyll gives access to hillside. Follow well surfaced track by stream up to Stickle Tarn. Turn right along E edge of tarn until reaching stream draining into tarn. Follow this uphill N, crossing it to go NW when track forks. This leads up stony rake with crags on left to top of fell, Pavey Ark.

Go SW on path around rim of crags left to Harrison Stickle. Climb down rocks W, then take path SSW, cross stream and curve W and then NW.

To reach next peak, Pike o' Stickle, a distinctive dome shape, go NW across grassy area and then scramble on choice of routes to summit.

Route is now NW over grass for 2.6km/1.6ml to reach Stake Pass just before a small tarn. Turn left to go SW on track, joining stream and zigzagging to valley bottom, Mickleden. Turn left on grassy then stony track leading to New Hotel, road and carpark.

This walk may be shortened after visiting Harrison Stickle. After crossing stream continue S. Large track with crags on both sides goes SE back to carpark. Save 5.6km/3.5ml.

85. Steel Fell to Helm Crag

Ordnance Survey Map No: 90 or OL Nos 6 and 7
Distance from city centre: 165km/103ml
Walking distance: 13.6km/8.5ml
Amount of climbing: 718m/2370ft

A ridge walk which I have found particularly attractive in autumn and where I have met relatively few other walkers, except on Helm Crag.

Park in Grasmere village. NY336073. To get there take M62/M6 to J36 and A590/A591 to Windermere and Ambleside. Turn left on B5287 into Grasmere 5km/3ml N of Ambleside. Pass church on right and take lane on left into carpark. Several other carparks in village.

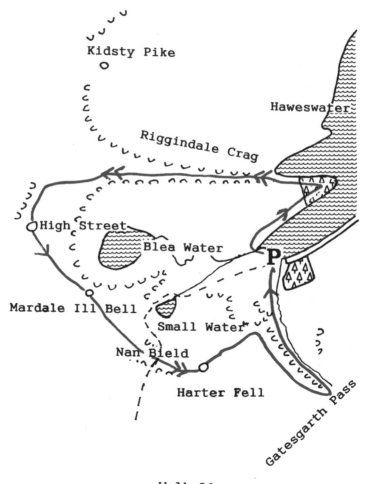

N

Kidsty Pike

Haweswater

Riggindale Crag

High Street

Blea Water

Mardale Ill Bell

Small Water

Nan Bield

Harter Fell

P

Gatesgarth Pass

Walk 86

From carpark turn left and take lane on right leading into village. Turn left on Easedale Road (signs for Youth Hostels) to Goody Bridge and turn right once over bridge. Ignore turning right over next bridge, and where lane bends right at Ghyll Foot keep ahead on bridleway to Helmside. Path now rises on ridge direct to summit of Steel Fell.

Follow line of old fence WNW, curving S past tarn and then over marshy ground to summit of Calf Crag, 2.4km/1.5ml away. Turn E then ESE to Gibson Knott, 2km/1.25ml away.

Helm Crag, last peak on ridge, lies 1.6km/1ml, E and then SE. Summit has several rock outcrops which can be climbed with care. Descent is by newly laid path going W from S end of summit ridge and zigzagging through crags to Easedale. It is well marked.

Go SE down Easedale to reach road back to Grasmere.

It is not practicable to shorten this walk.

86. *High Street and Harter Fell*

Ordnance Survey Map No: 90 or OL No 5
Distance from city centre: 184km/115ml
Walking distance: 11.25km/7ml
Amount of climbing: 894km/2950ft

The ascent of High Street from this remote valley is by a superb ridge where you may have the chance to see some of the few golden eagles in England. The course of a Roman road lies across the top and the smooth summits are supported by very craggy ground. Not for misty conditions.

Park at the S end of Haweswater Reservoir. NY469107. To get there take M62/M6 to J39 and B6261/A6 to Shap. At N end of village take minor road on left to Bampton. Turn left in village on road to Haweswater. Small carpark on right. Other parking in quarry to N.

From carpark turn right, go through gate and take right-hand path round edge of lake. Path doubles back

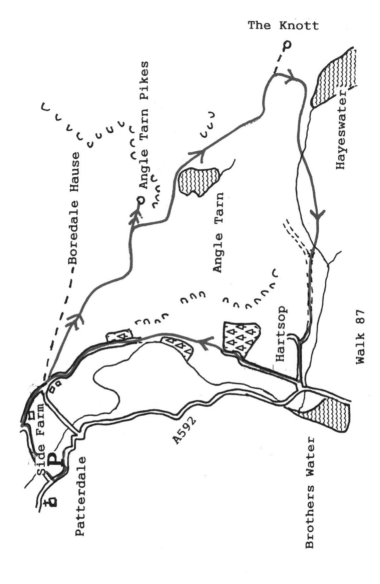

The Knott

Angle Tarn Pikes

Boredale Hause

Angle Tarn

Hartsop

Hayeswater

Walk 87

Side Farm

Patterdale

P

A592

Brothers Water

←N

just before wall and ascends ridge over crags direct to wall on summit. Turn left to reach TP. For Mardale Ill Bell go SE to edge of escarpment and follow round ESE with Blea Water below on left.

For Harter Fell go SE down to Nan Bield Pass (shelter in wall visible). Path beyond goes ESE and finally E to summit cairn with iron posts incorporated.

Descend to Gatescarth Pass by fence on right, going NE and then SE. Turn left at pass to reach carpark.

This walk can be shortened by dropping down N at Nan Bield Pass to Small Water. Path follows outlet stream to carpark. Save 2.5km/1.5ml.

87. Angletarn Pikes

Ordnance Survey Map No: 90 or OL No 5
Distance from city centre: 203km/127ml
Walking distance: 13.5km/8ml
Amount of climbing: 597m/1970ft

The twin peaks of Angletarn Pikes are very distinctive and are to be finally attained only by scrambling, although this can be very easy if you choose. The tarn itself is delightful to visit. Return is by Hayeswater and a valley path.

Park in Patterdale village. NY395160. To get there take M62/M6 to J40, A66 (Keswick) and A592 (Windermere) to Patterdale. Carpark on left just past school. Other carparks in Glenridding, 1.3km/0.8ml N.

From carpark turn right on main road and after 150m/170yd turn right to Side Farm at footpath sign to Boredale. Go through farm and turn right at sign. After going through gate, path climbs with wall on right above houses. *When path splits near seat take lower path.*

After 2km/1.25ml path crosses stream and turns sharp right. Summit can be reached by leaving path and going up to left. Choose own line up and down again to Angle Tarn. Continue with tarn on right. Path passes through cross wall and continues with wall on right though two more cross walls. Before reaching

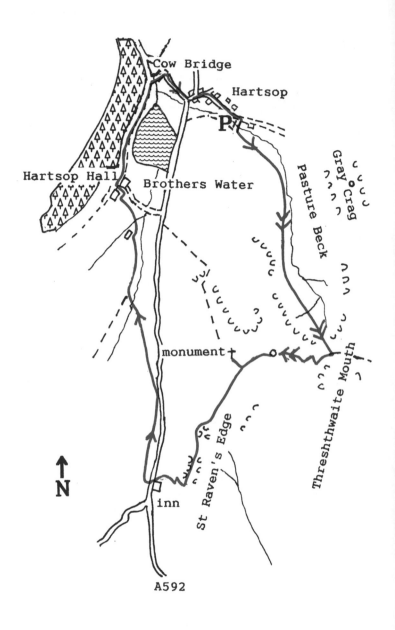

Cow Bridge

Hartsop

P

Gray Crag

Hartsop Hall

Brothers Water

Pasture Beck

monument

Threshthwaite Mouth

N

St Raven's Edge

inn

A592

Walk 88

next wall with steep climb up to The Knott, take path on right. This descends steeply S towards Hayeswater before turning W to go down valley to Hartsop.

Pass through village to last lane on right just before main road. Turn right to follow lane and then footpath. Keep on track to left by river where a path forks up to right. Outward route is joined above Side Farm.

It is not practicable to shorten this walk.

88. *John Bell's Banner*

Ordnance Survey Map No: 90 or OL Nos 5 and 7
Distance from city centre: 168km/105ml
Walking distance: 14.4km/9ml
Amount of climbing: 650m/2089ft

A mountain with a choice of names! The actual top is Stony Cove Pike and Caudale Moor also appears on the map. The ascent is up a valley with good rock scenery and a little mild scrambling from the col. The descent parallel to the A592 is better than it seems as the path soon draws away from the road and the stream deadens the sound of traffic. The track past Brothers Water is beautiful.

Park in Hartsop village. NY410129. To get there take M62/M6 to J36 and A591 (Windermere and Ambleside). At mini roundabout turn right on A592 to Kirkstone Pass. Just past Brothers Water turn right into Hartsop. Carpark at the end of narrow, metalled lane.

Go through gate at end of carpark, turn right at signpost for Pasture Beck and cross bridge. Track follows wall and then stream before climbing high above it as a path leading to wall across col, Threshthwaite Mouth. Turn right on path, following line of wall on right to plateau. Branch off to left to summit cairn on skyline.

Descend following wall on magnetic bearing 290°. After second bend on left look for monument to Atkinsons 100m/110yd on right. Follow wall over top of St Raven's Edge, ensuring that wall is on right before

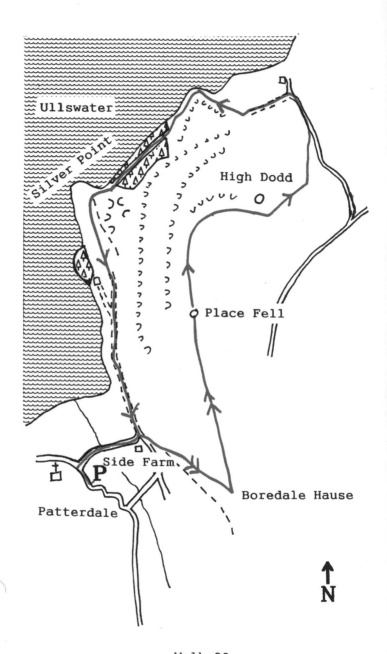

Ullswater

Silver Point

High Dodd

Place Fell

Boredale Hause

Side Farm

P

Patterdale

N

Walk 89

steep descent to Kirkstone Pass Inn (crags on right). Cross road into carpark and turn right to go through at far (N) end, picking up faint path following road on right. After signpost indicating permitted path to Brothers Water this is easier to follow. After crossing bridge climb half-right to join path just below tree line.

Go through gateway in front of second barn and turn right, following signpost directions. Cross bridge and turn right in front of barns and left through gate. Turn right on track passing farmhouse on right and then lake. Go through gate at end of track and turn right over old bridge (Cow Bridge). Turn right on A592 and take first left for Hartsop and carpark.

To shorten this walk continue NW past Atkinson monument on path which keeps to centre of ridge before dropping to right to avoid difficult ground. Turn right on A592 and watch for permitted paths close to road. Footpath on right leads to bridge and carpark. Save 4.8km/3ml.

89. Place Fell

Ordnance Survey Map No: 90 or OL No 5
Distance from city centre: 203km/127ml
Walking distance: 13.5km/8ml
Amount of climbing: 515km/1700ft

A day on this minor peak is worth while if only for the return by the lakeside path. It would be hard to disagree with Wainwright's view that it "is the most beautiful and rewarding walk in Lakeland".

Park in Patterdale village. NY395160. To get there take M62/M6 to J40, A66 (Keswick) and A592 (Windermere) to Patterdale. Carpark on left just past school. Other carparks in Glenridding, 1.3km/0.8ml N.

From carpark turn right on main road and after 150m/170yd turn right to Side Farm at footpath sign to Boredale. Go through farm and turn right at sign. After going through gate, path climbs with wall on right above houses. *When path splits near seat take*

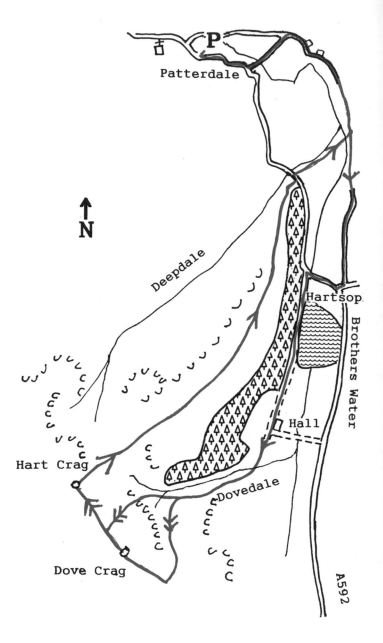

Walk 90

upper path. This leads to the col of Boredale Hause, marked by cairn and a few remnants of ancient chapel.

At Hause turn left to go N up ridge leading to TP on summit. Continue in same direction, heading for cairn with views over Ullswater before curving round E to col. Go S of High Dodd on track going NE down hillside to wall. Continue N to lane with wall on right almost all the way.

Turn left and after 500m/550yd turn left on bridleway signposted for Patterdale and follow lakeside on right. Where path forks near Silver Point go to right. Side Farm and outward route are joined past end of lake. There are alternative routes down N of High Dodd but they are no shorter.

90. Dove Crag and Hart Crag

Ordnance Survey Map No: 90 or OL No 5
Distance from city centre: 203km/127ml
Walking distance: 17.6km/11ml
Amount of climbing: 697m/2300ft

Although this walk does not stay on the high peaks for long, the descent by a long ridge gives ample views. The higher ground is very craggy and the walk is not recommended in bad, especially misty, conditions.

Park in Patterdale village. NY395160 To get there take M62/M6 to J40, A66 (Keswick) and A592 (Windermere) to Patterdale. Carpark on left just past school. Other carparks in Glenridding, 1.3km/0.8ml N.

From carpark turn left on road and on right-hand bend, turn left to cross river. At junction of tracks turn right to go S towards Hartsop village. Turn right at junction near village and right again on A592. After 0.5km/550yd turn left off road to join path. Turn left, passing Brothers Water on left. Beyond Hartsop Hall take right-hand fork, soon with wall on left.

The wall and fence which succeeds it can be followed to ridge and then right to summit. If you enjoy scrambling, take path skirting base of crags on right at point

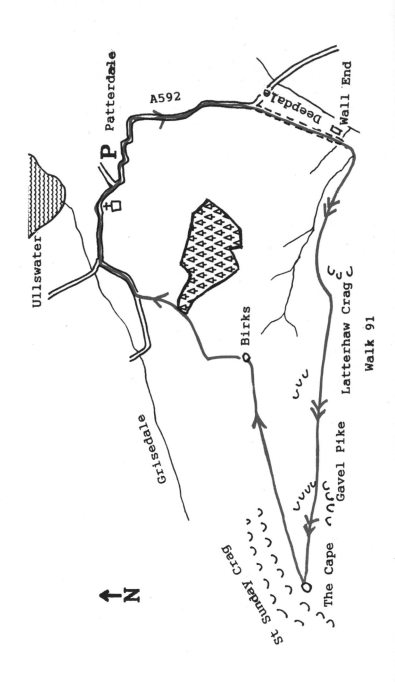

where fence turns S. On ridge turn left for summit of Dove Crag.

Hart Crag is 1.2km/0.75ml to NW and is by wall on left to a depression. Beyond, continue in same direction to summit cairn.

Descend by ridge to NE. At road turn left and after 50m/55yd, take footpath on right to bridge on far side of valley. Cross and turn left on outward route.

There is no possibility of shortening this route.

91. St Sunday Crag by Gavel Pike

Ordnance Survey Map No: 90 or OL No 5
Distance from city centre: 203km/127ml
Walking distance: 11km/6.8ml
Amount of climbing: 697m/2300ft

This is a less common route to a well known peak. Although no route is shown on map, a path has been worn and is easy to follow.

Park in Patterdale village. NY395160. To get there take M62/M6 to J40, A66 (Keswick) and A592 (Windermere) to Patterdale. Carpark on left just past school. Other carparks in Glenridding, 1.3km/0.8ml N.

From carpark turn left and walk on main road for 1.2km/0.75ml until a farm track goes off to right up Deepdale, the first valley, to Wall End. Cross stream by farm and a further stream. Turn up to right by this stream, passing sheepfold. Go right of Latterhaw Crag with stream on right. Above crag curve left to centre of ridge. Go straight up, W, to Gavel Pike and over a saddle to The Cape (name used only on map for summit of St Sunday Crag).

Descend NE for 2km/1.25ml over Birks and and then N and NE over rocky ground. Cross wall by stile and descend to lane. Turn right to reach main road and turn right for carpark.

It is not practicable to shorten this walk.

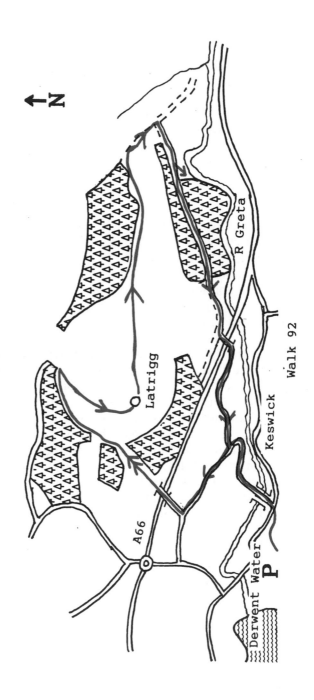

N

Latrigg

R Greta

A66

Keswick

Walk 92

Derwent Water

P

92. *Latrigg*

Ordnance Survey Map No: 90 or OL No 4
Distance from city centre: 210km/131ml
Walking distance: 10.5km/6.5ml
Amount of climbing: 290m/960ft

A favourite for all visitors to Keswick, Latrigg is another of those small hills which makes an excellent viewpoint and provides a good walk even on bad days.

Park in Keswick town centre. NY265233. To get there take M62/M6 to J40 and A66 to Keswick. Follow parking signs in town. Carpark is on left; another large carpark by lakeside.

Take alleyway NE from carpark into town centre, cross road and turn right. Road turns left and meets main road. Cross, continuing across river with Fitz Park on left. Road makes loop to right around site of old railway station. Take lane on right between fences (Cumbria Way) to cross A66.

Continue on path NE above wood and just before carpark at top of lane double back to go SW and around edge of steep ground to summit.

Turn left to go NE, cross stile and follow fence on left. Turn right at fence corner and turn right on track above wood. Take track E downhill to lane. Turn right and follow lane back over A66 to junction with outward route. Turn left back to town centre.

A better alternative is to take permitted path on left through woods, joining lane again just before A66 bridge.

This walk may be shortened by turning right at stile near summit and dropping down directly to A66 bridge. Save 3.5km/2.2ml.

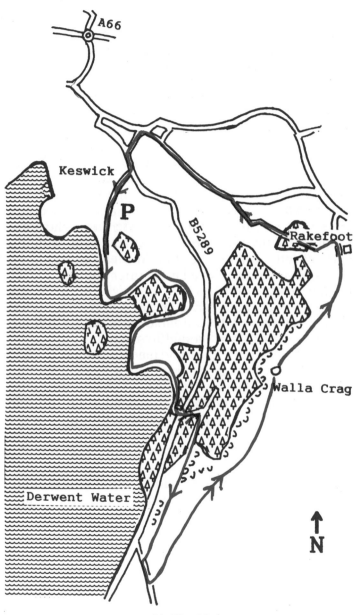

A66

Keswick

P

B5289

Rakefoot

Walla Crag

Derwent Water

N

Walk 93

93. *Walla Crag*

Ordnance Survey Map No: 90 or OL No 4
Distance from city centre: 210km/131ml
Walking distance: 10.5km/6.5ml
Amount of climbing: 303m/1000ft

A delightful lakeside stroll is followed by a stiff climb to the summit where views up Borrowdale and across the Vale of Keswick are superb. Good at all times of year.

Park in lakeside carpark in Keswick. NY265229. To get there take M62/M6 to J40 and A66 to Keswick. Follow parking signs in town, passing town centre carpark on way to lakeside.

Walk S past boat landing stages to end of lane and continue on lakeside path, coming inland where necessary and returning to lakeside. At S end of large bay, B5322 comes down to lake. Cross road and go up through wood into carpark. Turn right on to a path and follow sign to Ashness. This path traverses hillside going S and joins a lane. Turn left and near old gateway take path on left leading NNE to summit cairn. (For Ashness Bridge keep ahead on lane and return to gateway to resume walk.)

Follow wall NE down to lane at Rakefoot Farm. Beyond farm take footpath over bridge on left and follow path down through wood. This leads to lane and back to town centre.

It is not practicable to shorten this walk.

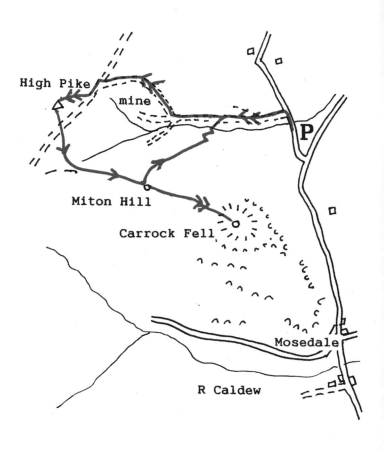

High Pike

mine

Miton Hill

Carrock Fell

Mosedale

R Caldew

P

Bowscale Fell

N

Walk 94

94. High Pike and Carrock Fell

Ordnance Survey Map No: 90
Distance from city centre: 206km/129ml
Walking distance: 11.25km/7ml
Amount of climbing: 518m/1710ft

This short walk has much of interest to offer the historian and the geologist. Rare metals have been mined in this area and the igneous rocks include the gabbro found on Skye. The summit of Carrock Fell also has the remains of an extensive hill fort. The route is mainly easy walking on old mine tracks and it is worth going on a fine day and spending some time looking around.

Park off the road N of Mosedale. NY350350. To get there take M62/M6 to J40 and A66 (Keswick). After 2.5km/1.25ml past junction with A5091 take minor road on right to Mungrisdale. Pass through village and then farm at Mosedale. Take unsignposted turning on left and park on large grassy area on right just before Ford sign.

Walk N on lane and cross bridge. After 100m/100yd turn left on stony track. Ignore fork to right and, where valley divides, two branches to left. Track climbs high through quarry spoil before turning left on to moor past open mine shafts. Turn left at junction with another track and after 200m/220yd turn to right uphill on path indicated by arrow made of post and stones. When path peters out maintain direction to summit (TP, shelter and memorial seat).

To descend, head S and a path develops shortly. On reaching track again, cross it on to path curving left to join a broader, grassy track. Head for distinctive cairn of Carrock Fell SE. Before beginning climb on to firm ground of Miton Hill note substantial track on left which is the way off. Continue over boggy ground and up through remains of ramparts of hill fort to summit cairn.

To descend, retrace steps over Miton Hill and turn right on track previously noted. This leads down to

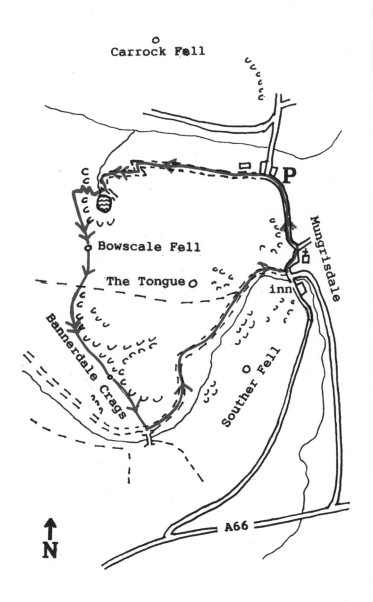

Carrock Fell

P

Mungrisdale

Bowscale Fell

The Tongue

inn

Bannerdale Crags

Souther Fell

A66

N

Walk 95

cross stream and joins mine track. Turn right for lane and car parking.

To shorten this walk turn left on track instead of ascending Miton Hill and Carrock Fell. Save 4km/ 2.25ml.

95. Bowscale Fell and Bannerdale Crags

Ordnance Survey Map No: 90
Distance from city centre: 202km/126ml
Walking distance: 12.8km/8ml
Amount of climbing: 497m/1640ft

These fells on the edge of the Lake District are relatively quiet and can offer good walking when bad weather affects more central areas. They are not to be under-estimated, however. Navigation is very tricky in mist and there are long craggy drops on the E. In his poem *Song at the Feast of Brougham Castle*, Wordsworth alludes to a legend of two immortal fish in Bowscale Tarn. Wainwright's *Northern Fells* contains an account of the spectral army of Souther Fell.

Park off the road N of Mungrisdale. NY359316. To get there take M62/M6 to J40 and A66 (Keswick). After 2.5km/1.25ml past junction with A5091 take minor road on right to Mungrisdale. Pass through village. Just before road takes sharp bend to right between buildings at Bowscale park on right.

Walk N on road to the bend and turn left on bridleway which leads all the way to Bowscale Tarn. Cross outlet stream on right and go up zigzag track between crags W of tarn to reach ridge. Turn left going SSE and then S to summit of fell. Descend SSW over boggy ground making for track on rim of Bannerdale Crags which then curves SE to highest point. Descend SE over grassy ground on gradually narrowing ridge to reach broad green track with stream beyond. Last section is steep. Turn left on track which follows stream and Souther Fell right to telephone box on road in Mungrisdale. Turn left to reach car parking.

To shorten this walk turn left on a track crossed

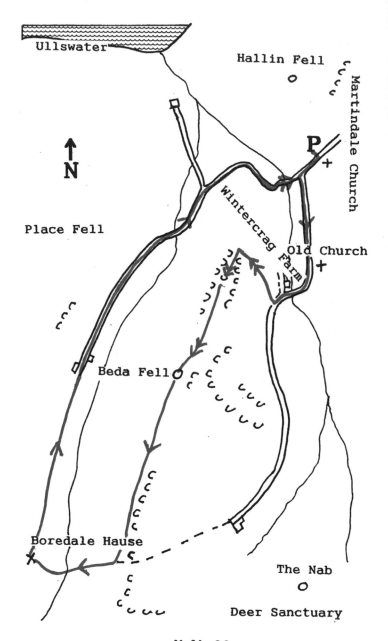

Ullswater

Hallin Fell

Martindale Church

P

N

Place Fell

Wintercrag Farm

Old Church

Beda Fell

Boredale Hause

The Nab

Deer Sanctuary

Walk 96

between summit of Bowscale Fell and track on rim of Bannerdale Crags. This runs S of The Tongue and joins main route 1km/0.6ml before reaching road. Save 2.5km/1.6ml.

96. Beda Fell

Ordnance Survey Map No: 90 or OL No 5
Distance from city centre: 198km/124ml
Walking distance: 11.25km/7ml
Amount of climbing: 429m/1415ft

Only the dedicated will know Beda Fell, a modest fell on the fringe of better-known hills which is not easy to get to. It is, however, the central point of the quiet and beautiful Martindale district, has an interestingly rocky scramble to begin with and is near a deer sanctuary. There are also two little churches and many people make the journey just to see them.

Park near Martindale church. NY436192. To get there take M56/M6 to J40 and A66/A592 (Windermere) and turn left on B5320 into Pooley Bridge at N end of Ullswater. Take turning on right past church and turn right at crossroads on minor road to Howtown and Martindale. Small carpark on right opposite church at top of col.

Go SW from carpark on lane and turn left at fork, passing Martindale Old Church on left on way to bridge. Cross and where lane bends left take path on right going NW across slopes of Winter Crag. (Avoid first path on right to Wintercrag Farm.) On ridge turn left to go S for scramble which leads to easier ground and Beda head, summit of fell.

Path now SW along ridge. Ground rises to small crag surmounted by cairn. A track crosses 400m/440yd beyond. Turn right on this track to go SW down to a stream. Then go NW to reach cairn on Boredale Hause (Walk 89) after 1.1km/0.7ml. Turn right, going NE. Path joins lane. When lane forks, go right, cross bridge and go up last slopes to carpark.

It is not practicable to shorten this walk.

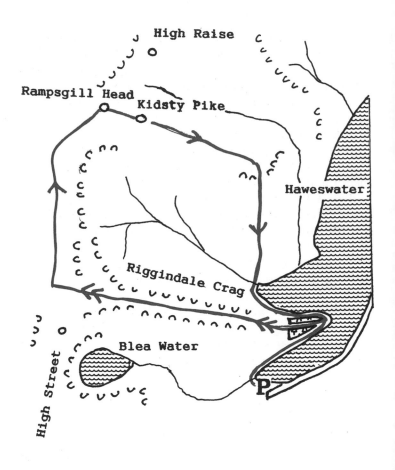

N

High Raise

Rampsgill Head

Kidsty Pike

Haweswater

Riggindale Crag

Blea Water

High Street

P

Walk 97

97. *Kidsty Pike*

Ordnance Survey Map No: 90 or OL No 5
Distance from city centre: 184km/115ml
Walking distance: 12.8km/8ml
Amount of climbing: 727m/2400ft
This walk shares an ascent with Walk 86 but turns N on the summit ridge to reach the remoter peak of Kidsty Pike whose distinctive shape is easily recognisable from the Pennines to the east. Not for misty conditions.

Park at the S end of Haweswater Reservoir. NY469107. To get there take M62/M6 to J39 and B6261/A6 to Shap. At N end of village take minor road on left to Bampton. Turn left in village on road to Haweswater. Small carpark on right. Other parking in quarry to N.

From carpark turn right, go through gate and take right-hand path round edge of lake. Path doubles back just before wall and ascends ridge over crags direct to wall on summit. Turn right.

Go N following wall on left down to col (Straits of Riggindale) before going NE up to top of Rampsgill Head. Go ESE for 0.5km/0.3ml with slight rise after depression to top of Kidsty Pike.

Cairned path leads E to end of ridge and then SE down to lake. Turn right on lakeside path back to carpark.

It is not practicable to shorten this walk.

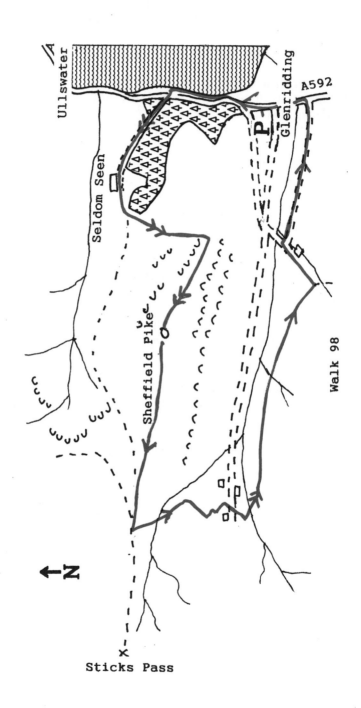

Ullswater

Seldom Seen

Glenridding

A592

P

Sheffield Pike

Walk 98

←N

Sticks Pass
×

98. Sheffield Pike

Ordnance Survey Map No: 90 or OL No 5
Distance from city centre: 182km/114ml
Walking distance: 10km/6.25ml
Amount of climbing: 567m/1871ft

This short walk is best not attempted in bad conditions as the fell is craggy on three sides. It goes through attractive woodland to begin with. The whole area to the W was the site of one of the largest lead mines in the area, finally closed off some 30 years ago. It is now being landscaped. Return is by route of old aqueduct.

Park in Glenridding village. NY386170. To get there take M62/M6 to J40, A66 (Keswick) and A592 (Windermere) to Glenridding. Large carpark right at S end of Ullswater.

From carpark cross road and turn left, going N on road until it is possible to walk by lakeside. Watch for stony track going up to left to cottages (Seldom Seen) 1.5km/0.8ml from carpark. Pass cottages on right and continue with wall on right to gate where walls join. Go through and turn left with wall and wood on left.

Traverse hillside when wall goes downhill to join path on SE ridge. Turn right (NW), climbing ridge to summit cairn. Continue W down to col and then take zigzag path SE down to valley. When path forks, go right and down to stream, turning left to footbridge.

Cross and turn left on to old aqueduct which traverses hillside. After path has curved right to go S, take track on left downhill at signpost. On reaching bridge, do not cross but turn right, following stream on left back to main road. Turn left for carpark.

This walk may be shortened slightly by returning along valley bottom instead of crossing stream. Save 0.5km/0.3ml.

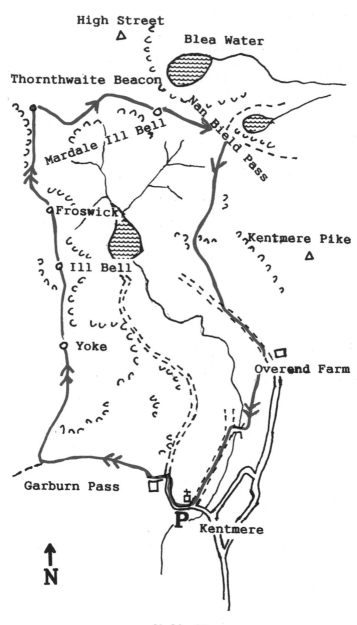

High Street

Blea Water

Thornthwaite Beacon

Nan Bield Pass

Mardale Ill Bell

Froswick

Kentmere Pike

Ill Bell

Yoke

Overend Farm

Garburn Pass

P

Kentmere

N

Walk 99

99. *Yoke to Thornthwaite Beacon*

Ordnance Survey Map No: 90 or OL No 7
Distance from city centre: 152km/95ml
Walking distance: 17km/10.5ml
Amount of climbing: 929m/3066ft

A splendid ridge walk to what must rank as one of the finest cairns in the Lake District, returning via Mardale Ill Bell and Nan Bield Pass (Walk 86) and a well graded path into the Kentmere valley. A hard day out.

Park in Kentmere village. NY456041. To get there take M62/M6 to J36 and A590/A591 (Kendal and Windermere). Turn right into Staveley 4km/2.5ml beyond Kendal bypass. Take minor road on right into Kentmere. Limited roadside parking near church.

From church go N. Main track goes ahead through gate, but turn left to farm and then follow signpost on right indicating packhorse track to Garburn Pass. At top of pass turn right and go through very marshy section with wall on right. When wall turns left keep ahead on ridge to summit. General direction of route is now N, keeping to top of ridge and passing over summits of Ill Bell and Froswick. From Froswick go NW at first before going N again, aiming for large beacon on Thornthwaite Crag, 1.6km/1ml away.

Section to Mardale Ill Bell is difficult in mist. Follow wall SE to its end and then go ENE to reach another wall corner. From here go E to Mardale Ill Bell. Descend SE and then E to Nan Bield Pass.

Take track S leading into Kentmere. Path turns SSE to reach bridleway in valley. At Overend Farm take right-hand fork to follow river. At top of rise cross wall on right by stile to reach bridge. Turn left on lane to reach church.

It is not practicable to shorten this walk.

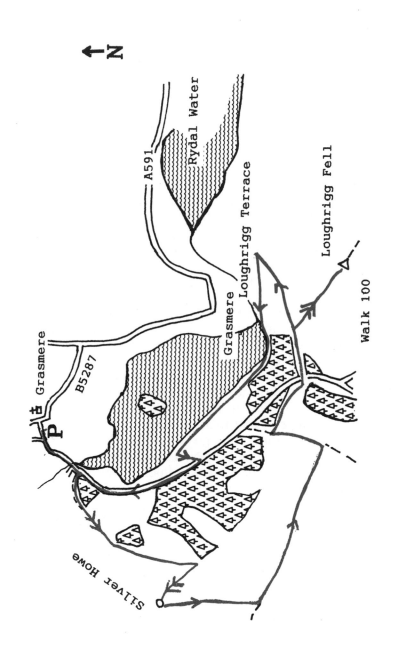

100. Silver Howe and Loughrigg Fell

Ordnance Survey Map No: 90 or OL No 7
Distance from city centre: 165km/103ml
Walking distance: 11.2km/7ml
Amount of climbing: 591m/1950ft

A low-level walk of great charm at all times of year. Specimen trees and small tarns add to the more obvious delights of Grasmere and Rydal Water and the surrounding fells.

Park in Grasmere village. NY336073. To get there take M62/M6 to J36 and A590/A591 to Windermere and Ambleside. Turn left on B5287 into Grasmere 5km/3ml N of Ambleside. Pass church on right and take lane on left into carpark. Several other carparks in village.

Turn left from carpark on lane going SW. After crossing bridge and just past boathouse on left, turn right by signpost through gate up walled lane through wood. Above wood there is no wall but another is soon joined. Walk with this wall on left until it turns sharp left. On this corner turn right and go NW uphill up a little scree gully and then to summit cairn on left.

Go S for 0.6km/0.4ml to reach cross track at point where ground falls away in front. Turn left to go ESE along highest ground. A large cross track joins with wood beyond. Turn left on this track but on reaching wall, go right with wall on left and then pass to N side of plantation to reach lane. Cross and continue between walls on Loughrigg Terrace almost opposite. At end of wall on right take path up to right, SE, to TP on summit of Loughrigg Fell, 0.6km/0.4ml away. Return to Terrace and turn right. Near corner of wood, path doubles back and drops down to lakeside. Turn left and follow lakeside path until it turns up to lane. Turn right for carpark.

This walk can be shortened by turning left on lane before reaching Loughrigg Fell. Save 3.5km/2.2ml.

AUTHOR'S COMMENTS
AND HINTS

Getting to The Start

It is no longer possible to reach the start of more than a handful of the routes in this book by public transport if a day trip is envisaged. A car or a hired coach, however, makes this a practicable proposition. Most of the routes outlined use the motorway network or the series of recently opened bypasses down the Welsh borders. These help to reduce travelling time, although I would advise leaving early in the morning, particularly on Sundays in summer. A car pool among friends will reduce costs considerably.

Wherever possible the parking area suggested is an official carpark provided by town or village authorities or National Trust or the National Park. Many of these are Pay and Display but for your money there are frequently toilets, refreshments and information points. Where this is not the case, please take care not to obstruct sideroads or gates into fields and for your own benefit watch for ditches hidden by long grass and do not park on soft ground. If there is a house or farm nearby it would be in your interest to let the occupants know that you are leaving the car intentionally.

Many country carparks now warn against theft from

vehicles. Leave nothing on view and take all valuables with you.

Clothing

There is scope for individual choice of clothing for hill walking but you must be prepared for much wider swings in temperature and other conditions than you would encounter off the hills. A combination of wind, cold and rain can be life-threatening and you must be prepared.

Footwear – in fine weather a few of the low-altitude walks in this book can be done in good quality trainers, although personally I prefer to wear lightweight fabric boots. The only real choice for mountains is leather boots with full bellows tongues and strong soles with good tread. Over-waxing can rot boots but they will need occasional treatment. Wet boots should be dried away from direct heat and with crumpled newspaper inside.

Outer-wear – the wind and waterproof anorak that is needed will also build up excessive heat and condensation inside and solutions of this problem can be extremely expensive. I would advise against buying the cheapest on the market and watching for sales of last year's models and colours – the market is now very fashion-conscious. On most models the zip fastening is covered with a flap closed by velcro. A hood is essential.

Mid-wear – shirt and woollen sweater are still used by many but the fleece jackets now available have many advantages. Again, if you don't mind last season's colours you'll find a better buy.

Under-wear – whatever your prejudices you will appreciate a set of thermals in winter.

Leg-wear – I find breeches convenient but they have never been regarded as essential in this country as they are on the continent. Old trousers or track-suit bottoms are adequate in summer, provided that you also have

over-trousers (see comments on anoraks). Gaiters are useful on boggy ground for keeping water out of boots.
Hat and gloves – you will need to carry both even if you don't use them all the time. In the cold carry a woollen or fleece hat and in summer take a sunhat if you suffer from heat. Woollen gloves and also waterproof mitts are useful.
Socks – all walkers used to wear two pair of socks but modern boots are usually well padded and one pair of loop-pile socks is enough for most people.
Spare clothing – sweaters, scarf etc. according to season.

Equipment

Rucksack – a wide choice is available but, again, bottom-of-the-market models are not durable. For day walks, 25 to 35 litres capacity is about right. Look for a model with two side pockets, a padded back and curved straps. Fit a cord grip if there isn't one and don't assume that the sac will be waterproof – use a plastic bin liner or something stronger inside.
Map – always have the recommended map with you and carry it in a map case or a freezer bag in bad weather. The legend on the map explains all about compass bearings, grid references and scales.
Compass – buy one of the Silva type with bearings in degrees. It is outside the scope of this book to give instruction in its use but all hill walkers will have to learn. The Ramblers' Association is currently setting up a standardised course which in a year or so will be widely available and there are already books on the market.
Whistle – buy a non-metallic one that will not interfere with the workings of your compass. The international distress signal is six regular blasts repeated at intervals of one minute.
Torch – I always carry a small one whatever the season, but in winter a larger one is essential. As a distress signal the pattern is the same as with a whistle.

First Aid – plasters, wound dressings and pain-killers are all that most people take. A group should consider taking more: several triangular bandages, insect repellent and Waspeze, antiseptic wipes, elastic bandages and knee/ankle supports.

Food and drink – according to taste! It is better to carry more food than you are likely to need as you will use a lot of energy during the day. At all events it is essential that emergency food is carried over and above what you plan to eat during the walk. This is best in the form of chocolate, Kendal Mint Cake etc., and will need replacing at intervals.

Other items – the list is endless, but you could consider the following: binoculars, a square of closed cell foam to sit on, a walking staff, particularly one of the new lightweight telescopic ones, a Swiss army knife, a pedometer, a short length of towelling to use as scarf or towel or to lay over barbed wire, an ice axe in winter and a plastic bivouac bag for emergencies.

On The Walk

Just how the day goes will depend on a number of factors. If you are on your own then you will not be bothered by somebody else's fast or slow pace. You should, however, limit yourself to safer ground, better weather and more familiar areas for safety's sake. Three or four in a group provides a margin of safety in emergencies but large groups, while they have their merits, are inevitably slower. If it takes one person 30 seconds to cross a stile and there are 23 stiles and 30 in the group, then it is not difficult to see how a large group will extend the time taken. Similarly, all the breaks seem to extend themselves and the leader has to plan for this.

A reasonable estimate of walking time for an adult may be made by allowing 12 minutes per kilometre plus an additional minute for each 10 metres of altitude to be gained (or 20 minutes per mile and 3 minutes for every 100 feet). Also allow a 10 minute rest for each hour of walking.

Other factors may affect your speed such as errors of navigation, head winds, rough terrain, minor emergencies. Allow for all this when planning the walk and enjoy the extra time in the pub if you don't need it.

Always make a final check of your equipment before setting off and, having done so, avoid the common mistake of rushing off at a fast pace. I have even seen people do this on the first day of the Pennine Way. By walking steadily the body will warm up before the big efforts are needed and have something in reserve at the end of a long day or if an emergency arises. Keep up a steady pace without too many short stops.

When you do stop, look for somewhere out of the wind and put some reserve clothing on. Mountain tops are not usually the best place for lunch but generally somewhere sheltered can be found not too far off.

Keep the party together whatever the conditions and however close the carpark. Accidents, great or small, tend to happen when you are tired, and a rush for the car is as likely a cause as any. In mist it is essential that you all keep close.

If I have made hill walking sound very daunting it is because I wish to stress that in bad weather and in winter conditions mountains are essentially a hostile environment, particularly for the urban creatures that most of us are. Planning, the right equipment, the right companions, fitness and experience will all help you to a state where the dangers are controlled and you can enjoy the many physical and aesthetic delights of the hills.

The Weather

I have already made much of this as it is such an important factor both for safety and enjoyment. If you take the advice given above you will have prepared for the worst. All you can do is check the weather forecasts and hope for the best. Air temperature falls by about

4°F per 1000 feet, whatever the weather, which is something to bear in mind when listening to weather forecasts. On the other hand, when the valleys are full of mist the sun can shine with brilliance on the mountain tops.

If you go out walking on a regular basis, don't be put off by the weather. It can often turn out much better than it is early in the day. Apart from that, if properly protected, walking in any weather can be enjoyable.

An accurate, local forecast issued by the Met Office and updated three or four times daily is available round the clock by phoning the following numbers:

Shropshire and Borders 0898 500 410
Gwynedd and Clwyd 0898 500 415
NW England 0898 500 416
Yorkshire Dales/Peak District 0898 500 417
Lake District 0898 500 419

Rights and Responsibilities

There has always been some conflict of interest between those who make their living from the land and those who use the countryside for enjoyment. At times I have been incensed by blocked footpaths, misleading or aggressive notices, by dogs, bulls and angry people. But not often. Farmers have a lot to put up with from some of the visitors they encounter and a considerate walker may get the backlash sometimes. I have met more helpful farmers than otherwise and have been grateful more than once for the initiative their wives show in selling tea and home-made cake. Many footpaths to the hills pass through a farmyard and rather than walk by in embarrassed silence try passing the time of day – you will usually meet with success.

The Country Code was devised to try to ease some of these tensions and it is worth repeating it here:

Enjoy the countryside and respect its life and work

Guard against all risk of fire
Fasten all gates
Keep your dogs under close control
Keep to rights of way across farmland
Use stiles and gates to cross fences, hedges and walls
Leave livestock, crops and machinery alone
Take your litter home
Help to keep all water clean
Protect wildlife, plants and trees
Take special care on country roads
Make no unnecessary noise

To the best of the author's knowledge the walks in this book are on rights of way or in areas where there are access agreements or on established routes that are not subject to dispute. In one or two cases permission has been given to walk over short stretches of private land where this facilitates a circular route.

In these cases in particular the walker is asked to take every care to avoid doing damage so as not to risk the good will that has been shown. Access agreements can be ended without warning and in grouse-shooting areas parts of some moors will be closed off on some days between 12 August and December. This does not affect rights of way and when I have met shooting parties I have always been approached courteously and the shooting area pointed out. It has not proved a problem so far.

In my view the walker's best defence against encroachments of the right to walk in the countryside is to join the Ramblers' Association whose address is:
1/5 Wandsworth Road
London
SW8 2XX
Tel. 071 582 6878.

INDEX OF PLACES